THE POWER OF PURPOSE

THE
POWER
OF
PURPOSE

LIVING WELL BY DOING GOOD

Peter S. Temes

HARMONY BOOKS/ NEW YORK

Copyright © 2006 by Peter Temes

Published in the United States by Harmony Books, an imprint of the
Crown Publishing Group, a division of Random House, Inc., New York.

www.crownpublishing.com

Harmony Books is a registered trademark and the Harmony Books colophon
is a trademark of Random House, Inc.

Library of Congress Cataloging-in-Publication Data

Temes, Peter S., 1966–

The power of purpose : living well by doing good / Peter S. Temes.—1st ed.

1. Success.   2. Conduct of life.   3. Interpersonal relations.   I. Title.

BJ1611.2.T42   2006

158.1—dc22   2005022251

ISBN 13: 978-0-307-33693-4

ISBN 10: 0-307-33693-X

Printed in the United States of America

Design by *Namik Minter*

10 9 8 7 6 5 4 3 2 1

First Edition

To Roberta and Lloyd, Eleanor and Irving,
and Judy, Katie, Leah, and Joe

ACKNOWLEDGMENTS

THE WISDOM OF MANY FRIENDS AND TEACHERS HELPED shape this book. Milton Kessler, Sidney Hyman, Joan Straumanis, and Malcom Brown have been the best of teachers. David Wagner, Joe Coulson, and Gerry Crinnin have been engines of inspiration over the years. Bernie Sucher was a generous reader of an early draft and a model of courage. David Ward and Marly Rusoff deserve particular thanks and gratitude for making this book happen. When I told David about the ideas I wanted to send into the world, he said, "Don't you have to write a book first?" Then Marly made it so. And through it all, Judy Temes remained my patient and wise partner. Thanks and love to all.

Four Lessons from Aristotle: Virtue Is Meaningless Unless You

    Use It to Achieve   46

Emerson's Struggle   49

4   **The Difference Between Ambition and Greed**   53

Ambition on a Global Scale: Owning What We Build Drives

    Us to Build Great Things   53

Against Greed: A Conversation with Michael Milken   57

Spiritual Ambition and Gimpel the Fool   60

PART III   INSIGHT: KNOWING WHAT GAMES OTHER
PEOPLE ARE PLAYING, AND USING THAT
KNOWLEDGE TO WIN

5   **Winning the War**   71

Always Focus on the War, Not the Battles   71

Sad Ice Cream: Missing Out on the Joy   78

A Lesson from Augustine: Fight *for* What You Love, Not *Against*

    What You Hate   82

Clarify Your Goals   84

6   **Knowing the Real Thing When You See It**   89

The Art of Reframing the Game   89

Know When You've Lost, and Turn a Battle into a War   93

Knowing the Real Thing When You See It   96

Lessons from Hannah Arendt: Thinking Critically

    About Yourself   101

Third-Level Questions for the Real Thing   103

Real Problems   106

7   **The Power of Purpose**   111

Be at the Center AND at the Fringe   111

Case Study: The Rise of the Internet   112

The Deal That Got Away: Understanding the Stronger and the

    Weaker   116

Case Study: The Hundred-Billion-Dollar Deal That
   Got Away   119

A Lesson from Plato: The Power of Purpose   121

The Leap of Faith: Connecting Insight to Relationships   129

The Greatest Prayer   133

PART IV RELATIONSHIPS: WITHOUT RELATIONSHIPS WITH OTHERS, NOTHING ELSE IS POSSIBLE

8   **The Three Critical Relationship Skills**   139

Share Every Gain   140

Giving and Taking   143

No Secrets   146

Secrets That Break Apart Teams   149

Finding New Glue for New Teams: If You Can't Sell Together,
   Sail Together   150

The Power of Poetry   153

From "Always Be Closing" to Always Build Teams   156

The Work Team   160

9   **The Power of Teams**   163

The Home Team   163

The Home Team Part Two: Showing Up   166

The Heart of One Community   172

Stanley Milgram: The Importance of Staying Close   174

Keeping Close: Pay Attention to the People Who
   Matter Most   177

The Three Elements of Successful Teams   180

Shared Commitments and Shared Interests   182

The Third Ingredient for Teams—What Is Shared Work?   184

Why Teams Fail   185

10   **How to Be a Truth Teller**   193

Lessons from Abraham Lincoln: Respect Your Opponent's
   Positions   193

Plato's Allegory of the Cave: How (Not) to Be a
   Truth Teller   198

Rehearsal Versus Real Understanding   202

Keeping It Real   204

A Lesson from Professor Brown   206

PART V   POSITIVE IMPACT: THE MOST WORTHY GOAL OF
ANY HIGH ACHIEVER

11 **Giving**   215

Why Give Your Time? To Help Others   215

The Trap of Looking Like a Hero (to Yourself)   218

Ideas: Sometimes the Most Valuable Help You Can Offer   220

Giving by Teaching   221

Money   225

Give to *This* School or Give to *That* One?   228

A Cautionary Tale: The Curse of $100 Million   229

The Gift of a Common Culture   232

12 **Where Does Purpose Come From?**   239

The Days Are Long, But the Years Are Short   239

Purpose Steers You Straight   242

Where Does Purpose Come From?   244

PART VI PUTTING IT ALL TOGETHER

13 **Making the Power of Purpose Work in Your Life**   251

Making It Work at Home: Family   251

Making It Work on the Job: Selling   255

Making It Work on the Job: Managing   259

Making It Work at Home: Community   265

Afterword: A Dream for My Children   271

Behold, I do not give lectures or a little charity,
When I give I give myself.

—WALT WHITMAN

PREFACE

THIS BOOK IS A FEW DIFFERENT THINGS AT ONCE. FIRST AND foremost it is a book about you—about helping you make your personal goals become real. It is also a book about service to others, the touchstone of meaningful success. And it is a book about ideas—some are ancient and enduring, while others come from the modern workplace, contemporary relationships, and the American family. There are a lot of ways to prove that these ideas work, as you'll see as you read on. But I know these ideas work at least in part because they worked for me as I set about to reach my own goals.

I began studying ideas about leadership and ethics—and how those ideas are connected—when I was a college student at the tender age of fifteen. But it didn't take at first. Though I started college early, I dropped out (twice, in fact). My wife's parents opposed our marriage—I was just nineteen at the time and had few prospects in their eyes, no degree, a flunky job, and the bad habits of hanging out in libraries and writing poetry in my free time. It was then that I began to study the forces that drive people to achieve ambitious goals—and my own goals certainly were ambitious. I managed to finish my college degree at night and talked my way through a back door to the graduate school at Columbia University while I was driving a taxi in Brooklyn. After taking a hatful of graduate degrees while working more than full-time, I landed at Harvard University as a junior faculty member (and I have to emphasize the word *junior*—I was about as low on the faculty totem pole as anyone without a broom in his hand could go). I was twenty-five by then, and my wife and I had two young daughters. I was proud of having made it to Harvard as a teacher—they certainly never would have let me in as a student—but the money quickly became a problem. The academic pay scale was modest, and I dwelled right at the bottom of it. I would look at my little daughters and begin to count the things I wouldn't be able to do for them unless I began making a fair amount more money. Finally I decided that I needed to take a step away from the university and focus on hard-core earning. I set a goal (one million dollars) and put a few of the ideas I'd figured out about success in business and life to use. I wrangled consulting work with major-league investment banks, consulting giants, and Fortune 500 corporations, including Goldman Sachs, Ernst & Young, and Citicorp. I also got involved in some Internet start-ups. In three years I hit my goal and then some. And then I put the next phase of my plan into action. I cut loose my clients, stopped focusing on money, and devoted myself to teaching and nonprofit work. Why kill the golden goose? Because all along, I had wanted to make money for only two reasons: to help my family, and then to help other people. That was the only way I could devote myself so fully to reaching my goals in the first place— knowing that it wasn't just about me.

INTRODUCTION

Can there really be a secret weapon, a special hook, an inside secret that the most joyful and successful people know and the rest of us don't? The answer is yes, and here it is: the more you focus on helping others, the more you will succeed in reaching your own goals. *Helping others is the most direct and effective way to reach* your *goals in your personal relationships, at work, and in your community. There is no better or more rewarding purpose you can find each day, and no more practical tool for getting where you want to go.*

WHAT DO YOU WANT? WHAT WILL MAKE YOU HAPPY? Ask people these questions—or quietly watch them go about their lives—and you'll hear and see a range of answers. People want success. They want control over their lives. They want money. They want love. They want to belong to communities that help them feel important and cared for.

But none of these desires is really an end in itself. It's not the money itself that people want—not the coins and the bills. It's what that money allows people to *do*. It's not power itself that people want, power sitting unused, but what power allows a person to *accomplish*. Even love and belonging are not truly ends in themselves—over time we learn that what is best about love is the act of *giving* love; what is best about belonging is the act of accepting others into the circle. The end point of our best desires is not selfish, not the *having* of love and belonging, but the *giving*. The great gift of love is the opportunity to show concern and caring, to help the ones we love. The great gift of belonging is to cherish the others in our circle, to express the power of the group through our own actions as individuals. This, in the final analysis, is what makes people happiest in the long run: helping others. It's what we do, not what we are. It's how we *give*, not how we take.

That's a simple enough principle. But it brings with it a powerful irony—one that can make a profound difference in what you accomplish in every aspect of your life. The more you focus on helping others, the more you will succeed in your own goals. Helping others is the most direct and effective way to reach *your* goals, in your relationships, at work, and in your community.

And that's what *The Power of Purpose* is all about—making the connection between reaching your own goals and reaching out to help others. Some find this the perfect and most logical path—*of course* helping others is the way to help yourself. Some see it as a contradiction—how can being focused on *others* help you? And some find the proposition troubling—they want their good works to stand on their own, unconnected to their own personal accomplishments.

But regardless of which position you hold—and even if you hold none of them—this book has a clear message for you:

make helping others your central purpose, and you'll do more good, find more success, and feel deeper happiness than any other purpose can bring you.

The Power of Purpose is a map for finding the confidence and power, the opportunities and occasions, and—most important—the techniques and strategies for centering your relationships and your work around helping other people. There is no better or more rewarding purpose you can find, and no more practical tool for reaching your own goals.

REACHING YOUR GOALS

What's the difference between reaching your goals and falling short?

We hear part of that question all the time—What's the difference?

Someone asks, Do you want vanilla or chocolate? Do you want to take the freeway or the back roads? Small coffee or medium? What's the difference, someone else replies, and those words speak volumes. Sometimes they mean "I don't care," or "I'm not paying attention." Other times they mean "I really can't tell what makes one choice better than another."

But the difference matters—a great deal. Ignore little differences in little things, and you'll find yourself settling for less than you deserve throughout your life.

What's the difference between the woman who gets no joy out of life and her neighbor who lives with tremendous happiness?

What's the difference between the worker who gets the raise

and the one who gets passed over? The one who makes the big sale and the one who merely comes close? The beloved character who cuts hair for tips and the woman who owns the shop?

What's the difference between the family in the cramped apartment and the family in the big house on the corner? Between the parents who fear their children are going down the wrong path and the parents who get it right? Between the people who make their relationships work, and those who grow old in isolation?

Can there really be a secret weapon, a special hook, an inside secret that the most joyful and successful people know and the rest of us don't? The answer is yes.

Aristotle knew about it and wrote about it (in ancient Greek—but there are translations). Most of the successful people you read about and see on television know about it, too—at least, the ones who are more than one-hit wonders, the ones who succeed time after time. Some people do in fact get lucky, but luck doesn't last. Only one thing does, if you're after real success in life: deserving it.

That's what Aristotle said—that happiness does not come from trying to make yourself *feel* good, but only from making yourself *be* good—from being a morally decent person.

And that's what the most successful people have that so many others don't: a dedication to helping others. These people win because they are stronger—mentally, physically, morally—than the people they compete against. Their strength comes from the greatest kind of motivation that exists, the desire to make a positive difference for other people.

The difference, it turns out, is all about looking in the mirror and saying this: "I can help others."

PART I

—

THE THREE LEVELS OF THINKING

1

The Three Levels of Thinking

Make the leap from asking, "who am I, and what do I want?" to asking that most powerful question of all—"how do others see themselves, and how can I help them feel stronger and more successful?"

GAMES ARE PLAYED IN ALL KINDS OF PLACES—SPORTS stadiums, backyards, offices, classrooms, kitchens, and dining rooms. But games are won in only one place—in the mind of the winning player. That's why Michael Jordan was consistently better than the tallest player in the National Basketball Association every year he played—having better physical tools to work with was not enough to beat a player like Jordan, thinking at a higher level. That's why some salespeople consistently sell more—of the same stuff to the same people— than the rest of their colleagues. That's why David slew Goliath, and that's why your personal path for your success begins right between your ears.

Here's the fact: how we think is the key to how we live. It's the key to your happiness, the key to your personal goodness, and the key to your success.

EAST VERSUS WEST IN THE PURSUIT OF HAPPINESS

One useful model of observation on how people think comes in the classic description of the difference between Eastern thinking and Western thinking. Begin with the observation that unhappiness is the product of unmet desires. Eastern thinking says, change your desires to match what you already have, and you will become happy. Western thinking says, change the world to fit your desires, and you will be happy. If you are unhappy because you live in a tiny house and want a bigger home, the traditional Eastern view would be to change your desire so that you want no more than you already have. The Western view would be to go out and build a bigger house, at almost any cost.

There's some wisdom in this model, but the world we live in today is no longer easily divided between East and West; each tradition has drawn on the other for decades now, and the habits and patterns of thinking of each have blended together in important ways. And in my experience, the most successful people have always combined elements of both traditions in their thinking—they embrace the ambition and outward focus of the West as well as the patience and humility of the East.

We all know people who are filled with the Western ambition to go out and change the world. Many succeed, at least now and then, by pushing against the forces of the world and reshaping them. But just about all of them also fail now and then—because they come face-to-face with people, ideas, or parts of the physical world that are simply too strong to be moved. And we all know people who are filled with Eastern patience and humility, ready to reshape their own desires to fill the world. At times, this approach to life is powerfully rewarding, with the ups and downs of the external world softened by a philosophical detachment from external things. But how many opportunities to make positive change in the world slip by, how many chances to have a real impact on the world are missed, because of this detachment?

But imagine the man or woman who looks at the world and understands, *this is when I should push, here is the opportunity to reshape the world in some small way,* and knows too when to say, *here is when I must step back, here is when my desire has to yield to patience.* The real power lies in being able to see *both* visions—both the ambition of the West and the humility and patience of the East—and being able to employ each when it best suits the challenge at hand.

Beyond East and West to the Three Levels of Thinking

For the world we live in today, the best model of human thinking I've come across is built of three levels or stages,[1] and it draws from the best of both the East and the West.

---

[1] Connecting the ways people feel and think with big-picture ideas about money is hard to do, but German economist E. F. Schumacher had a great talent for it. The three-level model of thinking is inspired by Schumacher's four-part model of human knowledge. As he got older—and more famous, especially in the United States—Schumacher began writing about larger issues in philosophy and psychology. In his book *Guide to the Perplexed* (a title borrowed from the great medieval Jewish philosopher Maimonides), Schumacher divided all of human knowledge into four categories. His ideas were at once abstract—hard to pin down in detail—and technical. But at their heart were the ideas that I've come to understand in terms of the three-level model of thinking.

At the first level, the most important question for understanding the world and taking action is How do I feel? or How do I look to myself? Picture a teenager waking up in the morning and saying to his parent, I'm not going to school because I don't feel well. Or the worker leaving a note on her desk right after lunch—Gone home, not feeling well. That's level one. How you feel about yourself is almost all you care about.

One level higher, the teen turns to his parent and asks, Do I look as bad as I feel? Or the worker decides not just to leave work, but to go talk with a colleague and say, Wow, I'm not feeling well. In reply, the parent may say, You look fine to me. Or the colleague may say, You should sit down and let me have a look at you. This is the second level, where you progress from asking How do I feel? or How do I look to myself? to How do others feel about me? or How do I look to others? This is a great leap forward—the individual is beginning to realize that other people are important, and that the ways other people see the world are important—but it's not remotely as powerful an outlook as the next level up, the third level.

At the third level, the central question is not about how I feel, or about how others feel about me, but about how they feel about themselves. That might seem like a small step forward, but it can't be overestimated. Think about a sales situation—at the first level, the seller is focused on doing a good job on her own terms; at the second level, she's focused on making a good impression on the sales prospect. But at the third level, the salesperson herself might as well be invisible, because she has no interest in looking good, but only in helping the sales prospect look good in *his* own eyes, and reach *his* own goals.

Or think about that teenager who doesn't want to go to school. The teen wakes up and says "I don't feel well" at level one. At level two, he's able to hear a parent say "you don't look sick to me." But at the third level, he's asking about how other people feel and discovers the best possible motive to get out of bed into the world: "other people are depending on me today." The motive to get up and out is not about what matters to *me*, but what matters to *others*.

In this is some irony, and some magic. Once you focus on others in this way—as a friend, as a citizen, as a manager, as a colleague—you find that you yourself benefit as much or more than the others you're trying to help. Focusing on the sales prospect's needs instead of your own, you eventually reap the benefits of greater sales—more money, more respect, more confidence. Focusing on getting up out of bed because you understand that you can help others—and what a transforming positive feeling that statement carries with it: *I can help others*—you find that you become healthier and happier. You help yourself as much as you help others, because your life becomes infused with the purpose of doing good.

My grandfather is a wonderful example of this effect. A self-educated man, he worked most of his life in jobs that did not satisfy his intellect or his desire to help others, but in his free time he was devoted to political causes that he thought could improve the lives of many. He was a socialist and an antiwar activist (though a veteran of World War II himself). Although some might argue that the specifics of his plan for improving the world were misguided, his personal sacrifices to help make positive change filled his life with a sense of purpose. I had the strong feeling that well into his late eighties, he continued to wake up in the morning and get out of bed in order to strike a blow against war, injustice, and poverty every day. That kept him healthy and engaged with the world while many others his age slipped out of touch. But my grandfather had a reason to live and to stay strong: he felt he was needed, and that he could help others.

A woman I know in New Hampshire has a similar story to tell. She calls herself a community activist, having worked for years to get the local government in her town to provide more services for young families and their children. She's spearheaded drives to create a free day-care center, to offer medical services for small children, and to give parents a safe and comfortable public place to bring their children when the long New England winter drags on. Sundays, she sets up out front of the local churches with her folding table, raising money and getting signatures on petitions. Weekdays, she sets up in front of schools and the one big food market in her small town. Everyone knows her, and she's got no shortage of critics as well as staunch friends—in small New England towns, there tend to be plenty of skeptics about providing public services, especially if they require tax dollars to be spent. But this energetic woman, a mother of two young children, says she loves her enemies. "Two things that motivate me," she says, "are helping the little boys and girls who need the basics and don't necessarily get them at home, and proving to those folks who don't think we ought to do more that *of course we ought to do more.* And I say this: thank goodness for those fools who don't want to help! They keep me fighting. If I didn't have such good and proper enemies, how would I know I was on the right track?"

She gets a good head of steam going as she talks. Clearly, this is a woman who sees her life as filled with important work. She is a hero in her own eyes—she's got to be strong to help the children in her area, and so she is strong. Cause and effect. Because she asks herself the fundamental level-three questions every day—How are others living? What do they think of as their greatest needs?—she's reaching ambitious goals, making an enormous contribution to the lives of others, and filling her life with high purpose.

THE THREE LEVELS OF THINKING

Getting past asking, "How am I? How do I feel?"

Getting past asking, "How do others see me?"

Arriving at the most important questions, "How do others see themselves? What are their most important goals?"

The commitment statement that leads to success: "I can help others."

THE STORY OF ED AND FRED: TUNING IN TO WHAT OTHER PEOPLE CARE ABOUT MOST

> *We all want to be our own heroes, and hear our own stories. If you grasp this truth, you can use it to reach your own goals.*

A famous story about the advertising business offers another glimpse of the way the three levels of thinking work.

Two advertising managers are arguing about the size of the type in an ad they're planning to run in a newspaper. One of them—call him Ed—wants to save money by using smaller size letters in the ad. Smaller letters mean a smaller, less expensive ad overall. The other—call him Fred—says, "You dope, you need big letters to catch people's attention. If we use smaller letters no one will stop and read the ad." Ed says, "Nonsense. If your message is the right message and you say it clearly, everyone will read the ad." Fred's not convinced. Ed proposes a wager: "I'll bet you a thousand dollars I can run an ad in tomorrow's paper that you'll need a magnifying glass to read, and no matter how hard you try, you won't be able to resist reading every last word." Fred smells easy money and takes the bet. The next day, the paper comes out and there on the back page is a block of tiny type. Fred laughs. "OK, pal," he says. "Pay up—I'm not reading it. I couldn't even if I wanted to—the type's too small." "Well, OK, if you really think you won't. But you should know what's in the ad. It's all about you. It's your life story." Try as he might, Fred could not resist, and before the day was over he'd gone out and bought a magnifying glass and read all about himself over and over again.

Fred was stuck at the first level of thinking—he was in love with his own story, as most of us are. Ed understood that and used his insight to win the bet and to save money on advertising by writing ads that used insight into the three levels of thinking to save on space. If you have no insight, your voice has to be loud to be heard—and your ads need to be big. But if you have lots of insight, your voice can be quieter and more civil, and your ads can be smaller and less expensive.

Ed was at the third level—he understood that other people didn't want to hear about the products he had to sell, or about him as a salesperson, but were consumed by their own concerns about themselves and their own personal struggles. He asked the right level-three questions—How do other people look to themselves? What do they care about most? Ed understood that if he could connect the sale of his products to those personal concerns, his ads would be more effective and he'd sell more.

The Three Levels of Thinking

THE STORY OF MARTY EDELSTON: HOW SECOND-LEVEL PRIDE HOBBLES THE CRITICS OF SUCCESSFUL PEOPLE

This is the story of a successful businessman with no shortage of critics. But his critics were at level one and level two. Marty was at level three. That's why the critics were working for Marty, instead of the other way around.

I first heard the story of Ed and Fred from Marty Edelston, the founder of a company called Boardroom, Inc. Boardroom publishes the newsletter *Bottom Line/Personal*, a title that has at times had more than one million paid subscribers. I first went to work for Marty when I was nineteen, and the experience was tremendous. It was a glimpse into big-time publishing and also a fantastic exposure to a successful entrepreneur just hitting his stride as his company was reaching sales of about $35 million a year. Marty is something of a legend in the publishing business, an idiosyncratic man with an iron grip on all the details of his company, requiring personal approval of every word published in his newsletters and books and signing off directly on just about every dollar spent. Throughout the day, secretaries bring Marty healthy snacks of sliced fruit, which he generally eats in the middle of meetings, with his fingers.

One of Marty's great talents is hiring bright and hungry people for key jobs. Many have publishing experience in more traditional firms and some are put off by Marty's highly personal approach and his total control of management at every level in the company. Executives used to running their own budgets and betting on their own best judgment sometimes feel suffocated. One wit on the editorial side who had come to

Boardroom from the *New York Times* once said, "Do you know what we're all doing here? All of us? We're just slicing Marty's fruit."

Successful people always attract criticism, little of it kind. In Marty's case, as in most, the criticism was not entirely wrong, but in some ways it was misplaced. Marty *was* autocratic—but his judgment was often better than everyone else's. Marty *was* rough around the edges—but he was also a remarkably decent and caring person. Marty *was* a pretty poor listener—but he was always honest and straightforward.

I worked for Marty twice, first when his company was about ten years old—that was the $35 million mark—and ten years later, when it was well over $100 million in sales and highly profitable. All those critics from ten years back, some of whom had gone on to work in big jobs at billion-dollar publishers, seemed a little silly when I got to see Marty's business sprinting along generating amazing amounts of cash and profits a decade down the road. It's not that their criticisms were wrong, but that Marty's vision was right in more important ways. He was reaching and exceeding just about all of his personal goals—he had millions in the bank, gave advice he believed in to millions of readers, employed all three of his children and his wife, and was treated with great respect by hundreds of people who knew him. I doubt that many of his critics had met their own personal goals so fully.

In the end, I came to believe that Marty's critics were driven by pride more than anything else. They would see themselves from an outsider's perspective and ask, What am I doing here slicing Marty's fruit? But Marty never once lost track of why he was in business—to help people. He had an absolute conviction that the information and advice he published were making a positive difference in millions of lives. There's no question in my mind that because Marty's truth was all about helping others, he was vastly more successful than his critics, whose truth was based on looking in the mirror, or imagining how others saw them, rather than serving others. The critics were at level one and level two. Marty was at level three. That's why the critics were working for Marty, instead of the other way around.

At the first level, the lens through which people see the world and themselves is the question, "Who am I and how do I feel?" This is what Marty's critics were asking themselves when, instead, they could have been focusing outward, putting their own identities aside and noticing what remarkable things Marty was accomplishing. This is the level of thinking a salesman exemplifies when he loses a sale but says to himself "I did a great job in there—the prospect just couldn't appreciate what I had to say." He's totally focused on how he looks to himself, not on making the sale or helping out his potential customer, and not learning what he can learn from others around him.

At the second level, the main question is "Who do others think I am, and how do they feel about me?" This level is exemplified by the parent embarrassed by his child's bad behavior in public, who then yells at the child so others watching won't think he's too soft on his kid. He knows it won't do his child any good, but he is totally focused on how others see him, so he plays the role he thinks others want him to play. Some of the people who worked for Marty were afraid to learn from him because they imagined their peers looking on, and they were embarrassed to be apprentices to a man who lacked the sophistication of their crowd—even though he was brilliant in running his company.

At the third level—the level where the power to reach your

goals lies—the main question is, "Who do others think *they* are, and how do they feel about *themselves*?" This level is exemplified by the parent whose child seeks her out for honest conversation. Why does a child *seek out* the contact with a parent that most parents are hungry for but can't make happen? Because the child feels stronger and more in control after talking honestly with the parent. What magic does the parent have that creates these feelings in the child? The parent's magic is that her focus is on how *the child* thinks and feels, not how *she herself* thinks and feels.

The same dynamic happens at work. The boss who helps her employees feel that they are reaching *their own* personal goals by getting with the company's program will win every time. Salespeople whose clients feel happier, smarter, and stronger when they come to call will build the kind of relationships that drive megasales, while the other guys are still checking their hair in the bathroom mirror. The magic comes from caring how the customer—or the colleague at work, or your child—looks to himself or herself, rather than how you look to him or her, or how you look to yourself.

Third-level thinking is all about helping others look good in their own eyes, and finding strength and happiness yourself by helping others feel stronger and happier.

The most successful people who worked with Marty were great level-three thinkers. They were focused on making their colleagues feel stronger and more successful—including Marty. Even on days he was overbearing, they understood that they were able to give him a gift by being humble and learning from him, even if his manners were rotten. In the process, these folks were able to learn from a master, make lots of money, and serve millions of people with a top-notch product. Not bad for a day's work.

2

THE CENTRAL QUESTIONS OF
THE THREE LEVELS

GETTING TO THIRD-LEVEL THINKING REQUIRES REAL strength; you'll have to resist plenty of people out there trying to keep you at the first level. A tremendous amount of energy goes into helping people function at that first level. Personal improvement gurus help people look in the mirror and feel good about themselves. Civil rights activist Jesse Jackson has spent decades teaching inner-city youth to say loud and proud, "I am somebody!" This is important work, without a doubt, but it is only the beginning—the first level. The next step is not to talk to yourself, but to listen to others—to begin to grasp that the way others see you is vital to you reaching your goals.

That will get you to the second level. And that's nothing compared with the power that comes when you reach the third level—the power to understand how others see themselves, and to help them feel stronger and closer to *their own goals* when they spend time with you.

Key Questions and Observations at Different Levels of Thinking

	Level One	Level Two	Level Three
Teenager	I don't feel well; I don't want to go to school.	I don't feel well; do I look sick to you?	People are counting on me—I'd better get going.
Manager	Am I a good boss?	Do my colleagues think I'm a good boss?	What do my colleagues and employees need from me to succeed? What are their goals?
Salesperson	I did a great job on that sales call, even though the prospect thought I was a jerk. I showed him that I knew my stuff.	I made a great impression on the prospect, even though I didn't get the business.	I learned about my prospect's needs—I'll make a bigger sale in the long run by building a relationship around what I learned today.
Parent	I know I'm doing the right thing even though I'm not getting the right results.	My neighbors and extended family know I'm a good, *tough* (or *loving,* or *involved*— whichever word is most important) parent.	I'm figuring out how to think like my kids think—that will help me anticipate problems and stop them before they start.
Community Member	I'm a great local citizen, even if no one agrees with me.	The right people agree with me, even though we're not getting much done.	I'm helping my neighbors come together, express their shared values, and make plans for the future.

Are these new ideas? Not at all. These ideas are the distilled teachings of thousands of years of human civilization. They are ancient and enduring, expressed in the literature of many cultures in many times and places.

In 1734, English poet Alexander Pope put these ideas into memorable words as part of his long poem "An Essay on Man." Pope wrote,

> *Man, like the generous vine, supported lives;*
> *The strength he gains is from the embrace he gives.*

"Embrace" here means two things—the vine embraces the fruit that grows upon it (that's a great metaphor for people gaining strength from giving practical help to others); and the vine holds tight to some support, a stake or a rockface or a tree. In this second sense, "embrace" means accepting support from others. So Pope is talking about man being strong by giving help and taking help at the same time; by inspiring faith in others, and by having faith in others. When our ambition is put in service of helping others, when our insight is put in service of the spark of precious humanity in every man and woman we meet, then we all grow stronger from the embrace we give, and our strength propels us upward.

Look again at the key questions for each of the three levels of thinking:

LEVEL ONE
How do I look to myself?
How do I feel about myself?
Who am I?

LEVEL TWO
How do I look to others?
How do others feel about me?
Who do others think I am?

LEVEL THREE:
How do others look to themselves?
How do others feel about themselves?
How can I help others?

Develop the habit of asking the level-three questions. Look hard at the clues other people give you about their personal goals and the ways they see themselves. Look for opportunities to help others feel stronger and more successful, and you'll see that you will gain as much as or more than others do. When you get past the zero-sum-game model of how the world works—the idea that for me to win someone else must lose—you begin to see the enormous power that comes from sharing your strength with others. That insight, and the moral strength that comes from helping others, are the greatest gifts you can give yourself, and they mark the clearest path to success.

To picture the three levels of thinking in high relief, imagine a weekend in the city. You arrive at the airport, where an old friend picks you up. You take a taxi to a hotel along with your friend, go out for dinner, get a good night's sleep, see a show the next day, and head back to the airport to fly home. Every interaction over the weekend happens at level one, level two, or level three.

It begins when you get off the plane. It's been a long flight, so you naturally think a first-level thought: I bet I look as bad as I feel, all rumpled and bleary. Then you see your friend, and you leap to the second level: how do I look to her? But the third-level thought is the best thought: how wonderful that she fought traffic to be here to greet me and managed to be here just as I landed. I bet she was waiting a long time; how lovely that she gave up most of her day just so I'd see a friendly face when I got off the plane.

You make your way to the taxi, and the driver reveals his level of thinking: if he's thinking at the first level, he'll be focused on his own internal concerns and might play that taxi-driver game of looking straight ahead while talking to people in the backseat, even when the car is just sitting there in the taxi line. If he's at the second level, he might make some efforts to be charming, to play the role of the taxi driver and look good in his passengers' eyes: "Welcome to the most wonderful city in the hemisphere, home to the smartest, fastest, and most beautiful citizens of the world" he might say, putting on a show. And it might be a fine show, worth a few minutes of attention and genuine enjoyment. But it's *his* show—it's more about how charming and funny he is than about what you and your host are doing or thinking. If the taxi driver is thinking at the third level, though, he'll begin with a question, rather than rehearsed patter. He might ask how you are, where you're coming from, what you want to learn about the city. If he asks honest questions and listens well, he might find some extra business in the process—perhaps taking you out to your restaurant, or taking your friend back home, or a return trip to the airport the next day.

At the hotel, things are much the same: the desk clerks might be stuck at the first level of thinking and offer grudging service because they don't like the fact that they have to serve others; they might put on a polished display of professionalism, impressive but generic, the same show they offer everyone; or they might listen carefully to you, make a real connection, and help you solve some of the little problems that every traveler confronts, from the missing tube of toothpaste to the need for simple advice about where to shop without paying tourist prices. If they're at the second level of thinking, when you ask for help with these things, they'll do a professional job in response. If they're at the third level, *they'll* ask *you* about those little things you might not yet realize you need help with.

The core issues never change. People who worry all the time about how they look to themselves will never be able to connect to others, and they will always be unhappy and unhelpful while they're stuck at the first level of thinking. People who tune into how they look to others will benefit from that awareness to a degree, but they will always be playing artificial roles and will miss the real opportunities to connect. These are the people at the second level of thinking. At the third level of thinking, people think about what others are thinking and feeling, about other people's needs, struggles, and dreams. Reach that level, and you'll connect powerfully with others, helping them reach their goals while you reach your own. That's the level at which life is sweetest, your personal relationships have deepest meaning, and your most ambitious practical goals—goals at work, goals about money—come within reach.

As your weekend ends and you head back to the airport, chances are you'll face no shortage of the usual challenges, from finding another taxi to getting a decent seat on your plane to taking off on time. At every turn, you'll face opportunities to connect to others and help yourself while helping them.

Will you undertake your journey as the hero of your own private drama, your own small world revolving around yourself? Or will you rise above that first level of thinking to see yourself through the eyes of others, tailoring your acts and words to make a good impression? That would be a step in the right direction. But best of all would be thinking at the third level, tuning into the dramas that others are living through, understanding what *their* struggles and goals are, and finding ways to help them look and feel stronger because of your brief presence in their lives. Do that, and you'll find that doors open in front of you, opportunities emerge when you least expect them, and the taste of life becomes sweeter.

GETTING BEYOND LEVEL TWO—FINDING THE FREEDOM TO FAIL, OR WHY MICHAEL JORDAN WAS THE BEST PLAYER IN THE NBA

> *The path to success is filled with failure. People who live their best and truest lives understand that. They are not afraid to fail, and not afraid of how they look to others.*

Michael Jordan was once asked to lend his image to an inspirational poster for schoolchildren. A well-motivated school publishing outfit wanted to put posters of Jordan in thousands of classrooms to inspire kids. Jordan was at the height of his playing career, and the publishers thought the image of his success would be a great inspiration to children struggling with their own challenges. Jordan liked the idea of reaching young people, but he didn't want his message to be about success—he wanted it to be about failure. "I've failed over and over and over again in my life," he famously said, "and that is why I succeed." That's the line that made it onto the poster and into the minds of untold thousands of youngsters.

Why the emphasis on failure? Because Jordan understood, as every high achiever understands, that the path to success travels through long fields of failure—that talent matters, but discipline and dedication matter more, in just about every field.

And he understood that the biggest barrier for many youngsters in reaching their dreams is fear of failure. Our culture emphasizes success to such a degree that we forget to teach about the necessary process of trying, failing, building strength from failure, learning lessons from failure, and then trying again.

Jordan's message was clear. He wanted to grab hold of the kids who would laugh at a schoolmate standing under a basketball hoop and putting up flawed shots that never find the net. He wanted to tell them, Don't you see? This isn't something to be ashamed of—this lousy playing isn't the destination, it's the pathway, it's the door you have to pass through to get to the place I found. And his message to every young person with a dream—every young person trying out life with a purpose—was to put aside the laughs from the sidelines, to put aside the bad guidance from foolish friends who say *Stop trying, you just look silly,* and focus on your purpose. Allow yourself to fail, and learn from your failings. There is no loss in failure if you learn the lessons failure has to teach.

Jordan's message was really about leaping past the second level of thinking. Put aside how you look to others. The path to excellence, the path to purpose, requires getting past that all-too-common question, *How do I look to others?* and focusing on your own determination to get where you need to go.

Second-level thinking keeps us from taking the risks we need to take to reach challenging goals. What kinds of risk does a young boy like Michael Jordan face bouncing his basketball and dreaming about a big future? Risks like this—*Will they laugh at me if I go practice my basketball game and miss more shots than I hit?* And we all face similar risks when we weigh the kinds of big steps that stand between where we are today and where we want to be—*What will they think of me if I quit my job and go out on my own? How can I go off to that great college when my friends and family think it's a waste of money? Why try to write my book when no one thinks I can pull it off? Won't people think I'm crazy if I walk out of my comfortable life to go work with poor people?* These are the questions that stand between most of us and our greatest potential, and they all center around that second level of thinking, where we keep asking ourselves, How do I look to others?

An American retiree named Eleanor told her story of getting beyond this second-level thinking this way: "People laughed at me and told me I'd never make it. . . . I was fifty-one at the time and everyone thought I was too old to make a difference. 'You've come too late,' they said." The people who laughed at Eleanor were friends and family at home, and new neighbors, local officials, and aid workers in Haiti, where she'd set up a new, free school for poor children. She had enough money to rent a five-acre school compound, but not enough for blackboards or chalk. She taught her first twenty students the alphabet by scratching letters in the dirt. From that difficult start, she build a school that now teaches six hundred students—students who would not be in school at all if she had cared too much about the people who thought she was crazy.

Another woman making a great difference in the world, Wangari Maathai, won the Nobel Peace Prize in 2004 for her work in building Africa's Green Belt Movement. Maathai organized tens of thousands of ordinary, mostly uneducated people to plant trees in areas in Africa at risk of becoming deserts because of decades of destructive agricultural practices. Maathai's vision for her movement grew out of her education—she was the first woman in the history of Kenya to earn a PhD in the sciences. As her understanding of the environmental problems in Kenya grew, she saw positive solutions to at least some of those problems. But she lived in a traditional culture. Her husband told her not to attract attention by agitating for change. Others said it was foolish for such a well-educated woman to work with people with no education or social prestige. Local government officials opposed her plans, rejecting (out of ignorance) her insistence on the importance of planting trees and telling her to leave the forest planning to government forest managers. People in her village thought she was crazy. Family members thought her education had ruined her. But she had a higher purpose and put aside her concern for how others saw her. The Green Belt Movement has, so far, planted thirty million trees in Africa, provided thousands of jobs to poor women, and revived traditional crops that help to strengthen the depleted soils of Africa. To make all this happen, Maathai had to put aside that question that comes naturally to all of us—how will other people view me?—and strive toward her higher purpose.

A woman I knew in Brooklyn, New York, faced similar challenges. She was an accountant, the first person in her family to finish college, and she was making a fine living working in a large business in a skyscraper in downtown Manhattan. Yet she was unhappy. She hated leaving her neighborhood every day and having to live so much of her life, as she put it, in a glass box in the sky. What she really wanted was to run a coffee shop in her neighborhood, to be one of those folks who knew everybody in the area, who kept an eye on things when others were away working. And she wanted to do something concrete and practical. "Do you know what I used to sell for a living? Numbers. Reports. Pieces of paper." Her knowledge of business gave her a great insight, though: coffee is one of the most profitable things you can sell. "I began doing research, and in some cases the cup actually cost more than the coffee. Ten cents for a fancy-looking paper cup, and at the low end, maybe eight or nine cents for a cup of coffee. And you could sell it for a buck, a buck fifty. There was a real business there for sure." But everyone she knew thought she was crazy, because accounting and office work were high prestige, and running a coffee shop was just another local gig. "I was one of the first people who grew up on my block to really make it into the white-collar classes," she said, "and people were proud of me. The fact that I didn't leave, that I kept living in this mixed-income area that I loved so much, made me much more visible. Now any number of folks I could name had jobs at this lunch counter or that coffee shop here and there—there was nothing in particular to be proud of doing that. But I would do it my own way. I'd do it right, and do it big." And she did. She now owns seven coffee shops in Brooklyn and Queens and travels to Central America every year to scout for the best coffee beans in the world. "I'm living the dream," she says, "because I understood that for all the love my people were giving me, I had to put aside how it might look to them if I took this leap. It was the right thing to do, so I did it."

Part of the magic of getting beyond the second level of thinking is that once you are past that level of thinking, you'll find it easier to take smart risks. People who take a gamble and win are generally looked at as heroes, while those who gamble and lose are looked at as fools. But as Michael Jordan made so clear, to get to a place where you win, you need to do a lot of losing first. You need to take the risks of doing new things, of investing your time and commitment and resources in crazy ideas like free schools in Haiti or new social movements in Africa or new businesses in Brooklyn or learning the tools of a new trade, if you want to get out of the usual lockstep lifestyle that rewards you with just enough, but never with all that you need to live the life you want to live. The rich might have money, the rulers of a society might have power, the well-born might have connections, but what everyone else has to level the field is risk—the choice to try something that might seem crazy, but to try it with a whole heart, with discipline over time, and without regard for how other people see you. Being different, challenging the old ways of doing things, and proving that there is always a choice to make your own path to success will be threatening to people who lack the courage to make their own good fortune. Getting beyond the second level of thinking frees you to put aside the opinions of the crowd, to take the kinds of risk that Michael Jordan took (how likely was it, really, that he would become the greatest basketball player ever? How likely was it that he would even be able to make a living as an athlete, when he was a skinny ten-year-old? After he was cut from his high school basketball team—and yes, he was—how likely was it that he would go on to become *Michael Jordan*? Every setback increased the risk he took as he charted his ambitious course—good risks, risks that make him what he was, and is).

If others didn't laugh at your dreams, if they didn't say "slow down; just wait awhile," if they didn't look at you a little funny when you said what you really believed, how different would your life be? What would you do differently? Would you be more like Michael Jordan, willing to fail and fail and fail to get to success? Would you be more like Eleanor, plugging away at a dream to help others even though everyone in your life told you you were crazy? Would you be more like your truest, best self?

The good news is that you can be there now. The trick is to

step past the second level of thinking by putting aside that question we all hear in our heads—How do I look to others?

Two Lessons from Michael Jordan

To succeed at any difficult, worthwhile task, you'll have to pass through a great deal of failure.

You must put aside the fear of looking like a failure in order to find your truest success.

Living Large at the Third Level of Thinking

Getting past the second level of thinking is vitally important. But where you get *to* is a bit trickier. Once you put aside how you look to other people, it's easy to lose your anchor and your sense of proper limits. After all, without the social limits that other people's opinions reinforce, what prevents us from acting selfishly? What guides us and gives us purpose?

Aristotle has an important answer to this question. Purpose, he writes, comes from the need to do things every day, to express our sense of right and wrong in the real world, among real people. We can't sit passively and be truly good. Real goodness is expressed in good *action*, not merely good thought. But this seems only a partial answer. What are the right things to be doing, those right actions we should be taking? Where do we get a sense of which actions are the right ones?

The best way to answer that question that I have ever found

is to look and to listen. Listen to the people around you. Look at the experience of others. The human experience is a profoundly social experience—we live by relating to others. And in that connection to others, we can find our balance. Right action is the action that helps others reach their goals and live better lives. Virtue is what serves the people we live among and helps them live better, happier lives.

How does this emphasis on others square with the idea that we have to stop asking, How do I look to others? That second-level question is, after all, a question that seems to be all about how other people feel. Yet second-level thinking is all about taking, and not about giving. It's all about putting limits on yourself—looking at how other people view you and using those views to tailor yourself to other people's values and expectations, to nip and trim yourself to fit other people's models. Second-level thinking centers on what not to do, on what is bad, on what should be avoided, on what to reject. It uses human connection to limit who we are and what we do, and it leads us to see the world as full of danger. We listen hard to what others think of us to avoid that danger. It's a fearful way to live.

And there are better ways to live. Human connection can be limiting, but it can also be freeing. Connection is more powerful and more joyous when it is based on a vision of a world that is infinitely expandable and full of wonder. And we can make that choice. We don't need to be smaller—which is what second-level thinking does to us, and to the world; it makes us smaller. We can, instead, be like poet Walt Whitman, who wrote, "I am large, I contain multitudes."

Human connection is in fact *more human* when it begins with the individual and moves outward. Rather than opinions of others pushing in on the individual, the third level of thinking puts the individual in the powerful position of *radiating out* with generosity. The leap from "How do others see me?" to "How do others see themselves?" is perhaps the biggest leap any of us can ever take. By turning our vision and our purpose outward, we open up to the world.

We become part of the world and all of humanity in a way that we simply cannot if we are always looking inward. By looking for the chance to give, by asking about the dramas and struggles that others live through, we live a richer life because we become part of a richer world. By attending to the happiness of others, we create a world in which our own happiness becomes, potentially, vastly greater.

Lessons from Quintilian: Even the Poorest Parents See Greatness in Their Children

The Roman philosopher Quintilian was one of the first writers ever to focus on what we can fairly call level-three thinking. Thirty-five years after the beginning of the first millennium—in the year A.D. 35—Quintilian was born in Spain, then a Roman colony. Quintilian was a professional orator and teacher, and he was accomplished enough that he eventually came to Rome, to work at the center of imperial power.

Quintilian wrote one book in his life, about education. Though he lived in a rigidly class-based society and came to Rome while a particularly cruel emperor ruled, Quintilian's writings show a great faith in human nature, and an instinctive belief in the innate potential of even the poorest children.

In his book *Institutio Oratoria*, he imagines himself, for the sake of argument, in the enviable position that Aristotle had held 350 years earlier, as the personal tutor of Alexander the

Great. "Let us suppose," Quintilian writes, "that Alexander were committed to me, and laid in my lap, an infant worthy of so much solicitude (though every man thinks his own son worthy of similar solicitude), should I be ashamed, even in teaching him his very letters, to point out some comprehensive methods of instruction?" It is Quintilian's passing remark here, in parentheses no less, that is most striking to the modern reader. In the democratic quarters of the twenty-first century, we take for granted that every parent does indeed believe his or her son worthy of attention and care as the royal conqueror of the known world. Yet Quintilian's brief comment was in fact a radical thing for any writer of his age to suggest—that every parent, even a man living in the muck of a Roman slum, will look at his child and see the potential for greatness.

Seeing children not through the eyes of the ruling class, not through the eyes of their teachers, but through the eyes of their parents is a great leap toward the kind of empathy and generosity of spirit that the most enlightened people of any age always possess. Every one of us is worthy of that kind of love and care, and when we cultivate the ability to see even the most wretched—or the most rotten—as their own parents might see them, we take a large step toward living a life of power and purpose, helping others while reaching and exceeding our own goals as well.

TWO LESSONS FROM QUINTILIAN

Even the poorest man sees in his child the prospect of greatness. Affirm his hopes, and your arguments will appeal to him.

Even the most wretched or rotten person is precious to *someone*. See through those eyes, and you'll take a great leap forward.

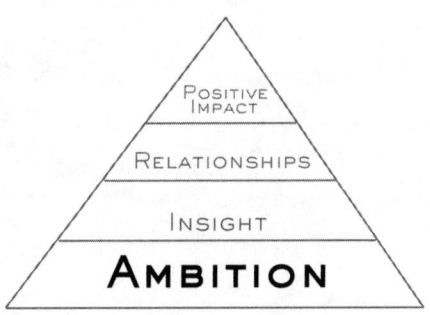

PART II

AMBITION: THE FOUNDATION FOR SUCCESS, AND THE ENGINE TO GET YOU WHERE YOU WANT TO GO

This chapter talks about Ambition, the first of four key ideas to the power of purpose. These ideas form a pyramid, with ambition at the base, holding the other three up. Without ambition, the others can't amount to much.

Ambition is the base—the foundation for success. Why? Because success is not an accident—you won't get it unless you admit that you want it, unless you sit up and tell yourself that you've got big goals and it's time to go out and get them. You'll still need discipline and patience, but ambition is the engine that will help you keep your passion hot and get you where you want to go.

*   *   *

We're often told that too much ambition is selfish, or even harmful. But ambition can be a beautiful thing—if it is driven by a concern for others, for having a positive impact on the world. Ask yourself why you want what you want. Is making money one of your goals? Why do you want the money—so you can spend it on yourself? Or are you thinking about using your money to help others, to do things like putting your kids through college, helping friends who need a boost, and maybe if you're very successful helping other people's kids get an education, too? Are you dreaming of buying a big new home? Why do you want it? To live in it alone? Of course not—not if your ambition is the kind that ends in real success and builds a positive legacy.

The kind of ambition that works in the long run comes from closing your eyes at night and dreaming of being strong enough to help others—of seeing yourself reach out your hand to support someone who needs your strength. That's what success really means—seeing someone in need, feeling the call of decency, and knowing that you can share your strength. Success means thinking and feeling and knowing, "I can help." That's the kind of ambition that makes a real difference in the world.

Ask yourself why you want what you want. Who will benefit from your success when it comes? If it's all about you, think about how you can draw a wider circle, how you can include others in your success. Think about what you can do to have a powerful positive impact on the world by using your success to help others. Committing to help others will help you find greater happiness on your path to success and in the winner's circle when you get there. And you'll be far more likely to get there—you'll be a stronger force as you fight on behalf of others, instead of struggling only for yourself. The best first step on the path to success is, in fact, to deserve it.

3

AMBITION DOES NOT HAVE TO BE SELFISH

> *Ambition need not be selfish. It can be as worthy as*
> *Mother Teresa's work—and frankly it should be. . . .*
> *The way to succeed is to play by the rules, but play*
> *harder and play smarter than the rest of the pack. Do*
> *that and you'll be on the side of the angels. Share what*
> *you gain, and you are doing the work the world needs*
> *done.*

A few years ago I had the pleasure of helping to create a degree
program in the study of leadership at a Catholic university near

my home, and I taught a number of courses in leadership there once it was up and running. I'd taught at other Catholic schools and was particularly interested in the views these students would have on leadership in the secular world.

The most interesting question I discussed with students there was about Mother Teresa of Calcutta. What, I asked the students, made Mother Teresa different from other nuns? We were all aware that in addition to the hospitals and hospices Mother Teresa had built in India, by her own count she had founded convents and schools in more than 120 countries. What did she have that the other nuns didn't, that drove her to accomplish so much in the material world?

The students had serious and thoughtful answers, but they all tended to point in one direction—the direction of piety. They would describe Mother Teresa bathing the feet of the poor, and their descriptions were passionate. Students, sometimes in tears, would offer images of Mother Teresa at work, the perfect image of self-sacrifice and humility. They would describe her simple, tattered saris, her personal modesty, and her acceptance of lepers and the near-dead as precious personal companions.

She was a holy woman, they would say. Her success was a product of her holiness. And I would never argue against that. But I would suggest that you could wash the feet of the poor for fifty years and not see any schools, hospitals, or convents built if you did nothing else.

In fact, one lesson of Mother Teresa's life was a lesson about ambition. Mother Teresa kept a fund-raising office in New York City (New York, to paraphrase a famous bank robber, was where the money was). And she was as likely to be on an airplane traveling on a fund-raising trip on any given day as she was to be in Calcutta washing anyone's feet. She also had a natural instinct for publicity.

So, what made Mother Teresa different from the other nuns? I make no claim to explain what was different in her soul or her spirit, but I can say without a doubt that what Mother Teresa had in abundance was ambition. She wanted to get things done and did not cease in her efforts to raise the money, to build the buildings, to fight the authorities who tried to stop her, until she had met her goals. And her goals were enormous, so enormous that she never stopped in her institution-building work. She was in love with the struggle to build more hospitals and schools and convents, and she kept at that work without letting up.

When you imagine an overfed fat-cat businessman picking the pockets of his customers and squeezing the life out of his employees, material ambition might seem like a nasty trait. But ambition is not ugly by its nature. It's not ugly unless you build your success on other people's backs. Don't let anyone fool you into thinking that that is either necessary or acceptable. Because ambition need not be selfish. It can be as worthy as Mother Teresa's work—and frankly it should be. You should never be ashamed of your love of success. Never be ashamed of your love of the game of getting what you seek. Never be ashamed of the powerful positive feelings that come from reaching your goals. The way to succeed is to play by the rules—but play harder and play smarter than the rest of the pack. Do that and you'll be on the side of the angels. Share what you gain, and you are doing the work the world needs done.

> **Three Lessons from Mother Teresa**
>
> Ambition does not have to be selfish.
>
> Ambition is most effective when it serves a greater good.
>
> Ambition can come hand in hand with modesty—the focus of attention can remain on the ambitious accomplishments and not on the ego of the person leading the charge.

Four Lessons from Aristotle: Virtue Is Meaningless Unless You Use It to Achieve

> *Real happiness is the function of years of doing the right things, of connecting your personal accomplishments with helping your family and your community be virtuous, too, day in and day out, until the very last days you've got.*

When you think about Mother Teresa, think about Aristotle, too. Bear in mind his teaching that happiness is not a psychological state, but a moral state. If you are unhappy, work on becoming a better person rather than chasing the feeling of happiness. In your personal life, if you are having trouble getting out of bed in the morning, don't try to convince yourself that getting out of bed will bring you selfish rewards ("If I get out of bed, I can go down and have some waffles and ice cream in the kitchen"). Focus instead on what you can do for others if you get out of bed, even small things ("If I get out of bed, I can check in on my buddy and see how he's doing—and then maybe we can grab breakfast together"). The connection between what's good for others and what's good for you is iron-clad: helping others helps ourselves.

In your work life, this means that if you're struggling to make a sale and feel blocked, don't focus on how you can close ("I can call and tell the prospect that someone else is bidding and he has to act now"), but on how you can add more value ("I can stop by and help him with the problem that's keeping him from focusing on completing the purchase").

As a community member, this means that if you're trying to change the zoning rules in your community to preserve open space, don't focus on the selfish virtues of your plan ("No one will ever be able to build new houses near you and block your views"), but on the collective gains ("With more open space, everyone's kids will know what it's like to have shared open space to play in, instead of every child being limited to her family's backyard"). The advantage in every case goes to the person who thinks about what others can gain from his or her own success. Doing what's good for the community creates a greater good for you personally. And it's not just the outcome that works for everyone, but the process, too. Day by day, inch by inch, the work of doing for others enriches your own life, pulls down social and emotional barriers, and helps you build a richer life.

Aristotle talks about these ideas in his book *Ethics*. He begins that book with an attempt to figure out what makes people happy. Pleasure is his first thought—things that feel good, that taste good, and that satisfy appetites lead to a kind of happiness. But this is a selfish and fleeting kind of happiness, and it does not appeal to those good things in men and women that separate them from animals.

So Aristotle then talks about honor: being recognized by others as a good and important person—being honored—makes people happy. Yet Aristotle knows that tying happiness to the whims of popular opinion is dangerous. The wrong people are often honored, while the best people are often neglected or despised.

That leads Aristotle to the idea of virtue—happiness, he says next, is about being virtuous, being good. But a person could be good all day long and not get anything done. Aristotle is a big believer in action over passivity; his larger philosophy rests on the idea that truth is expressed by people doing the things they are good at. So virtue *in general* is less appealing to Aristotle than virtue *in action*. Actually going out and getting things done is a vital piece of the puzzle, and so Aristotle says that "not only complete virtue, but also a complete life" is necessary for happiness. By "complete" he means full of activity and accomplishment. He also means that a man or woman can only be completely happy at the end of his or her life—that it's not enough to have a good day or a good year. Real happiness is the function of years of doing the right things, of connecting your personal accomplishments with helping your family and your community be virtuous, too, day in and day out, until the very last days you've got.

"Always," Aristotle tells us, a happy person "will be engaged in virtuous action and contemplation." Always is a long time, long enough to do good and to reflect upon what the good *is*. Getting on that path today—and staying on that path for the long run—are what bring happiness and success, according to the founding mind of the Western tradition.

FOUR LESSONS FROM ARISTOTLE

Happiness is a moral state, not an emotional state.

If you are not happy, seek to be a better person instead of simply seeking to feel happier.

Being good means doing good. Virtue is useless unless it leads to positive action.

Help others to be happier by helping them to become *better*.

EMERSON'S STRUGGLE

Ralph Waldo Emerson's worldview was always generous and filled with hope. But it took a great personal loss for him to reshape his ideas and emphasize doing over thinking and feeling.

Aristotle's focus on action—on the *doing* of goodness rather than simply *being* good—is especially important in light of the struggles that most of us go through in our lives. In a world that is simple, a world that is always kind and never brings hard news and sad events to ordinary people, perhaps it would make sense to be good in a passive way. But in a world like ours, in which we all face struggles of various kinds, the active mode of being good is often what keeps us from giving up in the face of adversity.

The story of American philosopher Ralph Waldo Emerson offers a clear example. Emerson was a young writer and minister with a happy life when he published his first collection of essays and lectures, *Essays, First Series*, in 1841, and his work is bursting with optimism and happiness. In that book, the essay "History" is perhaps the most important, creating a spiritual and intellectual framework for his other essays, including the more famous "Self-Reliance," which captured the American spirit of do-it-yourself prosperity that was to become a model for American culture for the next hundred years. "Every man," Emerson writes at the beginning of "History," "is an inlet to the same and to all of the same." That means, to Emerson, that there is a universal human spirit that we all share—one great spirit and one great intelligence that we can all tap into. "What Plato has thought," Emerson says, any individual "may think; what a saint has felt, he may feel; what at any time has be-fallen any man, he can understand."

These are no small claims, but Emerson makes them feel real. And he really loves the individual—he has tremendous faith in the importance of every man and every woman. His essay is a celebration of how powerful and important the individual is. "He should see that he can live all history in his own person," Emerson writes of the common man. "He must sit solidly at home, and not suffer himself to be bullied by kings or empires, but know that he is greater than all the geography and all the government of the world; he must transfer the point of view from which history is commonly read, from Rome and Athens and London to himself. . . ." He really believes that the individual is the center of the universe. If this sounds a little like the kind of passive virtue that Aristotle tried on but eventually rejected, that's about right. Sitting solidly at home and contemplating how important one is, the very center of the universe, is a far cry from Aristotle's final prescription, that the virtuous man or woman go out to do things that help others in order to make virtue real.

Emerson's personal circumstances were just as comfortable and his prospects were just as promising as you'd expect of a man with such a self-satisfied philosophy. He was married to a lovely young woman, lived in a large, comfortable house in Concord, Massachusetts, in the center of a group of deep thinkers who thought of him as a great spiritual and philosophical leader. He was regularly invited to visit churches and lecture halls around the country, and he was becoming a national celebrity.

But then something tragic happened. Emerson's five-year-old son—a boy he dearly loved—died of scarlet fever. His next set of essays, published in 1844, contains a piece called "Experience," which I think is really a new version of "History." In the intervening years, though, Emerson has lost all his optimism. He begins "Experience" this way: "Where do we find ourselves? In a series of which we do not know the extremes, and believe that it has none. We wake and find ourselves on a stair; there are stairs below us, which we seem to have ascended; there are stairs above us, many a one, which go upward and out of sight. . . ." Emerson says it plainly: he is lost. Where his view of history, that great abstraction of the collective human spirit, was brimming with joy in 1841, before he had known deep personal pain, by 1844, after the loss of his son, Emerson thinks in much smaller terms. History has shrunk to experience. The universal man who would share ideas with Plato and feelings with the saints now stands teetering on a staircase, like a drunk waking up from a blackout, not knowing where he is, how he got there, or where to go next.

With this bleakness, though, also comes a kind of resolve. Through the pages of his essay, Emerson thinks through the choices that men and women face in our common world. "I am very content with knowing," he writes toward the end of the essay, "if only I could know." By this he means that he would be delighted to enjoy, again, that passive virtue that Aristotle rejects—the enlightenment of sitting and knowing truth and goodness without having to get up and actually do things. He *would* be content with that, if only he could still feel those feelings. But he can't. The experience of personal tragedy has robbed him of that easy kind of happiness, and now, to cure himself of the bleakness he portrayed at the beginning of his essay—waking to discover that you are halfway up a staircase, not knowing what to do next—he has to rouse himself and become active. In a world without suffering, he could sit and think and feel, but in a world that has pain as well as pleasure, he must rise up and make things happen, he must *do* as well as *be,* because doing is the only cure for the darkness of the soul that his personal losses have caused.

"Up again, old heart!" he writes at the very end of "Experience." "There is victory yet for all justice; and the true romance which the world exists to realize, will be the transformation of Genius into practical power." This is a profound revelation for Emerson. He is saying that he was wrong in his first essay, naive. Now he understands that the world is more than an intricate flower expressing the complexity and beauty of the human mind. It is a place of struggle, a stage on which great acts must take place. The great destiny of man is not only to reflect and understand, to think and feel, but to do practical things, to build and create and make great things happen. Only action will lead to real happiness, and real goodness. The easy satisfactions of the philosopher who wants to think all day must be transformed into the tools we can use to get practical things done. Only then can we get past our sorrows; only then can we find greatness.

4

THE DIFFERENCE BETWEEN AMBITION AND GREED

AMBITION ON A GLOBAL SCALE: OWNING WHAT WE BUILD DRIVES US TO BUILD GREAT THINGS

You might know the name Hernando de Soto—but chances are, you're thinking of Hernando de Soto, the Spanish explorer who charted large areas of Central America, the Caribbean, and the American South in the sixteenth century.

The *other* Hernando de Soto is an explorer not of the high seas and undiscovered countries, but of ideas. De Soto, an economist in Peru, had devoted his life to a big question—Why does capitalism generally produce good results in Europe and

North America, but not elsewhere in the world? This might seem like a pretty abstract question—like a matter of politics and economics without much meaning in the lives of ordinary people who live in countries with sound economies. Yet de Soto's answer to his big question about world capitalism touches everyone, and it explains a lot about how and why we wake up early to go to work, how and why we care about the things we own, and how and why we dream about our futures. The key, for de Soto, is property. More specifically, the key is property rights. Every man and every woman needs to have the government recognize what he or she owns. You and I might take that for granted, but imagine how different our lives would be if we could not prove that we owned our homes, our cars, or even the clothes we wear. De Soto makes the connection between ownership and work very clear: if we could not own what we work for, we would not work as hard for it, and we would all live less well. Not only the rich would suffer without clear property rights, but the poor, too. The poor *especially*. Property, de Soto tells us, is itself a source of social justice and uplift for the poor. We should never feel that our ambitions to own what we work for, to save, to build, to buy, somehow come at the expense of the poor. Indeed, those instincts to save and to build and to buy are precisely what help the poor become less poor, so long as the governments they live under help them record and protect what they own.

And this is not just a theory. De Soto is not talking about what might happen. He is talking about what does happen, in the majority of the world, in those many countries where the governments do not keep clear and honest records of who owns what. Two case studies illustrate his point. In Haiti, many private homes sit on publicly held park land. When a family builds a home and moves in, they tend not to invest time and money in building it sturdily, in modern plumbing or electricity, or in any of the other things that would help bring that home to first-world standards of living, in part because they know that they'll never have clear legal title to the home, and therefore when it comes time to sell it, they won't be able to get a price much higher than the basic building materials cost. In many cases, when families in these houses move, they simply abandon their homes. Because most of the poor don't have a functioning system to establish property ownership, their property can't be bought and sold with confidence. And because of *that,* people don't invest time, labor, and money in assets that they can't sell for a fair price later. But, de Soto says, if people were given clear title to their homes and the land they sit on, a wave of great investment at the grassroots level would begin, and living standards would rise.

Another case study de Soto likes to use is the city of Cairo, in Egypt. For decades, Cairo has had a severe housing shortage; demand for new homes is enormous. When new buildings go up, they usually rise to five stories. But within a few years, they sprout two or three more—families scavenge building materials and build unofficial homes on top of the buildings. But because the homes don't officially exist, or officially belong to anyone, they can only be sold for a fraction of what they would be worth if they were officially recognized. Because of that cap on what they can be sold for, the people living there can't borrow money to improve them and generally don't invest the time, labor, and money they'd need to make them safe and sanitary. But, de Soto says, if title to these properties were given to the people who build them—perhaps on condition that minimal safety standards be met—a wave of investment would dramatically improve the lives of the people who live there.

De Soto extends his ideas beyond housing, to the vast unofficial economies of underdeveloped countries ranging from illegal taxi services, unsanctioned hospitals, and hidden-in-the-home restaurants to squatter-farmers who can't invest in long-term agriculture because they farm land that does not belong to them, and they must be ready to flee the authorities at any moment.

Grant legal status to all this "informal" economic activity, de Soto says, and a burst of ambition and entrepreneurial energy will begin to raise living standards in poor countries. Let poor people own what they build in clear and uncompromising terms, and they will build great things. Let them invest their time and their sweat in making their own lives better, and the lives of many others will improve, too—success, in the end, is contagious. De Soto teaches that the West has had a head start in modernization because philosophers like John Locke of England and political leaders like Thomas Jefferson in the United States made the connection between individual liberty and the idea of property rights. Locke wrote that every man is his own property—that he did not belong to any king, but to himself. He also wrote that the only moral justification for ownership was the investment an individual made in improving what he owns. Jefferson echoed many of Locke's arguments in the Declaration of Independence and turned the abstractions of the philosopher into the foundations of a new nation. Jefferson's commitment to the freedom of every individual to think and believe as he or she wishes, to act in the public sphere without fear of government oppression, is directly connected to de

Soto's belief that the right to own what we build unlocks the freedom of even the poorest citizens of the poorest countries to dream big dreams and to work hard to make them real.

These freedoms fuel ambition. They free us to dream, and they challenge us to accomplish great things. Our ambitions honor these freedoms and pay tribute to thinkers like Locke and Jefferson.

TWO LESSONS FROM JOHN LOCKE

Property is a fact—everything is owned by somebody.

To deserve what you own, you need to invest time and energy in making it better.

A LESSON FROM HERNANDO DE SOTO

Owning what we build drives us to build great things.

AGAINST GREED: A CONVERSATION WITH MICHAEL MILKEN

> *Celebrating ambition and success does not mean defending greed and dishonesty. It's not about being like the business-people who do a few months in country-club prisons and then return to Park Avenue. Instead it's about making a genuine contribution to society, and playing by the rules, but playing harder and smarter than the competition.*

It's not hard to find people who will tell you that becoming wealthy is morally wrong, that being a boss is inherently unfair, and that reaching all your goals means that others will be deprived of their own success. Unfortunately, this has been true too often in the past. There are plenty of abusive and selfish millionaires out there. But there are even more whose success has been the key to hundreds of *other* people's success stories. Economic success is not always virtuous, but if you commit to reaching your goals ethically—by working harder, being more insightful, and relating to others more skillfully—and you dedicate yourself to use your economic strength to help others, you'll do more good with money in your pocket than you could with empty coffers.

At its best, this philosophy can free you to achieve more, and to use your achievements to help others. At its worst, this philosophy can be a fig leaf, a cover-up for flat-out greed. I once had a conversation with the onetime billionaire and self-admitted felon Michael Milken that seemed to me to represent the height of the fig-leaf philosophy—an ugly view that we must all reject if we are to be worthy of our own success. Today, Milken devotes a great deal of time to nonprofit work, particularly leading research efforts to cure prostate cancer, and he deserves great praise and respect for that work. He is also heavily involved in education reform, both as a philanthropist and through new for-profit business ventures. But the Milken that much of the world remembers is the man who largely invented the world of the junk bond. In the 1980s, Milken was an investment banker working out of an office in Beverly Hills, making deals for companies that other bankers would not touch because they were not financially sound enough to earn investment-grade ratings from the firms that evaluate the quality of bonds. Before Milken, big-time investors—often pension funds, school endowments, and other big institutions—were very conservative lenders. They bought bonds in blue-chip companies, not start-ups, not companies trying to move from one line of business to another, or trying to enter entirely new fields. The investors wanted a modest return on sure bets. That was the big-time bond investing game.

Milken changed the rules. He created the market for bonds in shaky ventures by convincing the issuers to offer very high interest rates. The big potential returns drew in investors who, one hoped, knew they were taking big risks but were willing to go along because they got such a high return on their investments. Some on Wall Street hated Milken for changing the rules of the game they'd been playing to their own satisfaction for decades. Others called him a hero for opening up new sources of capital for high-risk ventures and funding waves of high-risk innovation that would help bring new companies into life, new technologies to the marketplace, and new millions to the pockets of bankers and executives at the center of all these deals. But there was more to Milken's deals than inventing junk bonds. He ultimately confessed to financial crimes that had nothing to do with the quality of the bonds he was trading, but everything to do with misrepresentation and fraud.

I bumped into Milken in the lobby of a New York City venture capital firm at just about the height of the Internet bubble, when he was visiting VCs to talk about his own postprison business holdings. I was in transition from the private sector to heading a nonprofit, and Milken and I spoke about how nonprofits can have their greatest impact. "But never forget," Milken told me, "that by running a business you make a great contribution to society, too, by employing people, generating trade, paying taxes." I smiled and agreed. Of course, he was right.

But I was suppressing the urge to ask him whether he had reflected on that idea while spending twenty-two months in federal prison for the five criminals counts that he had pled guilty to (originally he'd been charged with ninety-eight criminal counts and made a deal to get that down to five, along with a $200 million fine. If the fine seems steep, note that in a single year while he was committing financial fraud Milken earned $550 million). And these were not victimless crimes. One of the victims, in fact, was my mother-in-law, a physician who immigrated to the United States from Hungary and scrubbed toilets for a living during the years before she mastered English and earned her U.S. medical license. Some of her retirement money was in an account with an insurance company called Executive Life, a client of Milken that was tipped into bankruptcy in part because of his financial crimes, costing my mother-in-law part of her hard-earned money.

So when I talk about sharing every gain, about dedicating your success to helping others, and succeeding ethically, there's more to this than good PR. It's not about being like the businesspeople who do a few months in country-club prisons and then return to Park Avenue. Instead, the models for success are in every town, from every background, of every race, ethnicity, and religion—the folks who've made their money by playing by the rules, but playing harder, playing smarter, and playing with the kind of values that not only help you reach success, but help you deserve it.

SPIRITUAL AMBITION AND GIMPEL THE FOOL

> *Truth matters—though at its root, truth is something we feel, rather than something we can prove.*

The Difference Between Ambition and Greed

If ambition is a search for something you have not got—a search, often, for money, for power, or for privilege you don't yet enjoy—perhaps the most important kind of ambition is *spiritual* ambition, the yearning to understand the difference between illusions that can fool us into living our lives badly and the aspirations that can lead us to the most meaningful, positive kind of existence. Put more simply, spiritual ambition is the search for spiritual truth.

Any number of people will happily tell you that they have the truth all figured out, and that all you need to do to get some is to sign on to their view of the world. And plenty of people *do* sign on and find some comfort in the answers that come prepackaged and readily consumable. But one of the distinctive aspects of the age we live in, particularly in the Western tradition, is skepticism about truth. Modern science is built on skepticism, on the demand that truth prove itself to be real, and science certainly proves its worth every time we take healing medicine or marvel at a skyscraper. And very few spiritual truths stand up to hard-core skepticism. Say "prove it," and they vanish in a puff of air. But without some notion of truth, our lives go untethered. We tend to drift and lose all sense of right and wrong.

Even worse, without truth to guide us, raw power takes over. Lewis Carroll captures the way power fills the vacuum created when truth vanishes in a famous passage from *Alice in Wonderland*:

> "When I use a word," Humpty Dumpty said in rather a scornful tone, "it means just what I choose it to mean—neither more or less."

> "The question is," said Alice, "whether you can make words mean different things."
>
> "The question is," said Humpty Dumpty, "which is to be master—that's all."

Alice makes the commonsense reply to Humpty Dumpty. She wants to know how he presumes to make words mean what he wants them to mean—to say that one thing is another, that the sun is a pie, that a hand is a foot. She seems to feel what most of us feel, that words really do have specific meanings, that they connect to the things they represent, that there's a true link between the word and the thing, even if the thing is abstract, not a foot, say, but beauty, or love. Alice is clinging to the idea of truth—that we live in a world of real meaning, and that the job of language is to help us communicate that meaning.

If you say there is no truth, how can you say that a word like *beauty* means anything beyond what a bunch of people get together and decide it means? That's Humpty Dumpty's position—that words don't have absolute meanings. They mean what he says they mean—that's his power in action. This is what Humpty Dumpty seems to mean when he says that "The question is . . . which is to be master—that's all."

And language is only the beginning—without truth, nothing has any fixed meaning. Just as words go about meaning whatever the strong want them to mean, every other aspect of our lives might as well follow the path of power, or the path of pleasure, or no path at all. If you can't prove that one path is truer than another, why bother to do anything that doesn't feel good in the moment?

In the end, there is no way to argue against this kind of bleak philosophy, a philosophy that celebrates nothingness and the vanishing of the human spirit. But that turns out to be good news, because argument is not the point. The most important truths, in the final analysis, are not a matter of proof or argument. They are felt rather than known. They require heart as well as intellect to grasp. So the fact that you can't prove to Humpty Dumpty that some things are right and others wrong, that words have real meaning beyond what you might want them to mean, is not a real problem. Instead you weigh his assertion that words mean what he says they mean, and you can reject it because you understand that the world is made of more substantial stuff than that, even though you can't prove that fact with any precision. You know he's wrong, that he is missing an essential quality of how the world works, even though you can't hold up that quality and say, here it is. The truth in this case is something you experience but don't control.

And this, it turns out, is the most powerful position to hold—the most human, most hopeful, and most effective in helping each other build meaningful and satisfying lives: to know that truth exists, but also to confess that we do not hold it in our hands; that truth is what we strive for, what we feel, but have not captured.

That's the balancing point between no-truth and all-truth—the *path* toward truth. It is certainly a core idea to the Western tradition. The Greek epics are all about journeys, and not nearly as focused on conclusions and arrivals. And Eastern traditions embrace similar ideals. In the Chinese text the *Tao Te Ching*, we read that "The enlightened possess understanding / So profound they can not be understood." The enlightened understand the truth—that truth is real. But they cannot tell you what it is. You've still got to take your own continuing journey to truth; you can't just read about someone else's. So you might be heartened in your dedication to the truth, given evidence that your journey toward truth is toward something real, but what, exactly, that real something might be, you've got to keep journeying on to discover. That is what ambition of all sorts can do for us—keep us moving forward.

A wonderful short story by the writer Isaac Bashevis Singer, "Gimpel the Fool," makes this point with the style of an old European storyteller. Gimpel is a sad-sack resident of a small Jewish community in rural Poland—a *shtetl*—and he suffers no end of misery at the hands of just about everyone he meets, from his childhood friends to the leading citizens of his community to his wife. But even in the face of years—decades—of abuse, he retains great dignity and hope. "No doubt," Gimpel says near the end of the story, "the world is an entirely imaginary world, but it is only once removed from the true world." In that simple statement is a powerful philosophy. Gimpel tips his hat to the modern thinkers who say that truth is impossible to find or to prove. Indeed, we cannot hold out the truth and say here it is. Our world is, alas, a mirage. Should we then give up hope, give up joy, because we are living a lie? Not at all, because the truth is out there—it might not be exactly right here, but it's close. Only once removed from where we are right now, in fact. Close enough that we can feel it. Close enough that we can put up with the sad fact that our world is merely a dream, because it is a dream awfully close to the true world. That our world is imaginary should make us humble, and help us realize that our knowledge will always be incomplete. We should never be too satisfied with the satisfactions of this imaginary world. That we are only once removed from the true world should make us sit up a little straighter, take our hopes and dreams—and the hopes and dreams of others—that much more seriously. Humpty Dumpty turns out to be wrong, in Gimpel's world. There is a true meaning to words, and a true meaning to human existence. We can't quite express it, because we're not quite in the true world yet, but we know we are close.

In a way, spiritual ambition is a lot like poetry. Poetry is the art of expressing the inexpressible, of using words to come as close as humanly possible to saying what can't be said. We've all had feelings we can't quite put into words. Poetry takes that "can't quite put into words" quality and gets just a little closer to putting it, only once removed. This is the joy of poetry, and the joy of life—it takes a little faith to feel how close to the truth we are, when we can't really prove it. But the lesson of Gimpel is that even without proof, the truth is real.

Singer wrote "Gimpel the Fool" just after World War II, as the awful news of the concentration camps was filtering out into the world. Singer, who was born in Poland, came to the United States in 1935, missing an awful fate by a few years. He of all people would have good reason to look at the world and say it is not just, not sensible, and perhaps not real. But his story was an important statement of hope. Even without proof of some governing truth to our lives—and even in the face of so much horrible evidence that the world is cruel—Singer tells us, through Gimpel the Fool, that there is something bigger, truer, and more important than what we see around us. He offers us the greatest kind of spiritual truth—hope, even in the darkest times.

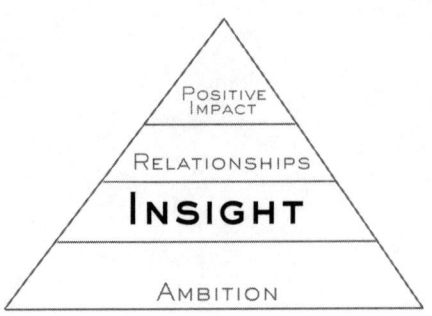

INSIGHT: KNOWING WHAT GAMES OTHER PEOPLE ARE PLAYING, AND USING THAT KNOWLEDGE TO WIN

Insight is the second level of the pyramid. Building on Ambition, Insight helps you get where you want to go with fewer diversions and potholes. It's all about knowing what games other people are playing, and using that knowledge to win.

The most successful people I know understand that the two most important goals—helping others win, and seeking to win yourself— are really the same goal. You win the biggest victories yourself by helping others win. Being their trusted ally is a more powerful position than being the last man standing after a battle. Instead of winning a game that has taken a toll on all players, you get to redefine the game to focus on building alliances instead of destroying opponents.

Understanding the three levels of thinking is vital to winning these victories. By now you've had some time to mull over the three levels of thinking. That is a crucial insight, and as you use it to understand the people you live with and work with, it will provide you with great practical opportunities to come closer to your goals.

In addition to that one big insight, a number of smaller insights are also important to help you get where you want to go.

One of the most important is to focus always on the war, and never on the battle—always on the long-term goal and never on the short-term victory.

Another is to blend conservative thought with radical thought—to be at the center and at the fringe at the same time.

Knowing where you stand in negotiations of all kinds—whether you are the stronger party or the weaker—is also vital.

And finally, understanding how far reason can take you, and how to take a leap of faith when reason's power fades, are absolutely essential if you are going to reach your personal goals at work, at home, and in your community.

5

WINNING THE WAR

ALWAYS FOCUS ON THE WAR, NOT THE BATTLES

The easiest victories are the petty ones. The truly important victories are few and far between. The critical insight is that the short term never really matters—winning battles does not win wars.

It's one of the most common mistakes people make in their personal relationships and in their jobs—giving in to the urge to argue every time you're contradicted, and to win little victories over others every chance you have. Winning these little victories certainly feels good in the moment, but a person with insight will feel just fine losing lots of battles while winning every war.

Everyone likes to win—and not just once in a while. People like to win *all the time*. But most victories come with a cost. The easiest victories are the petty ones. The feeling of power that comes from making a clever, cutting remark or proving yourself smarter than someone else is a petty victory. The victory that comes from dominating a discussion or taking advantage of a friend or colleague is a petty victory.

The truly important victories are few and far between. They have little of the short-term emotional payoff of the petty victory, but they bring great rewards. *The critical insight when it comes to winning and losing is that the short term never really matters—winning battles does not win wars.* North Vietnamese General Giap understood this during the American war in Vietnam when he said that "For every defeat the Americans suffer, we will suffer ten. But they will tire first." The Americans can win every battle, Giap was saying, but the Vietnamese will win the war.

And, of course, it is only the war that matters. Salespeople know this all too well. How many have celebrated getting the lead, and then winning the pitch, winning the first stage of a sales process, and then the second, and then the third, and then losing the sale in the end? The battles didn't matter; the war was where the money was.

Many divorced people know this—how many won every argument but lost their marriages?

Job applicants know this. You can ace the interview but still not get hired. Parents know this. You can get your kids to dress well and speak respectfully but still watch them make foolish life decisions. And we all know that we can win an argument and in the process lose a friend.

This straightforward concept—focus on the war, not the battle—has many practical applications. Perhaps the most important is understanding when *someone else* needs a victory. Locked in conflict, we all have the same emotional fight response that makes it hard to ask this crucial question: what if I let this other guy win? He'll feel better—he'll feel like he's won and I've lost—and his good feelings will help me to get closer to *my* long-term goals.

Vivid examples are easy to find in family dynamics. A thirty-something man tells this story, a clear example:

I was in love with a beautiful, accomplished woman. We'd been living together for almost a year and were starting to talk about marriage. She made me very happy—but also drove me crazy. She wasn't careful around the house, and I just hated to see the cap off the toothpaste, the refrigerator door left open a crack, all those little things. And I know I drove her crazy, too, less because of what I did than because of what I didn't do. I'd ignore her when she made me angry, because I didn't want to fight. But then she'd be so offended that I wasn't talking to her, she'd really blow her top, and cry and yell.

And I felt I was right. I *knew* I was right. You *have to* close the fridge door or the food spoils and stuff melts and you get a flood on the floor—but I was losing something bigger. I really loved her. I thought I was right about the little things, but finally it occurred to me that maybe there was something else I wasn't right about, something in how I dealt with her when I was angry. So I called her at work one day, and I laid it all out. I told her I thought I was right about the toothpaste and all that but that I wasn't loving her enough, caring about her enough, and that I was going to work on doing better. That on the bigger issues of why she was mad at me, that I was wrong and she was right. And man, it was like a key turning in a lock. She just opened up and everything got so incredibly better. She'd felt, I think, that I hadn't really given her all of my respect before, and my saying she was right and I was wrong—something I was kind of trying out, really, something I kind of almost believed—totally changed that, and we got to a higher level. Everything got better, and all the time since then has been the happiest in my life.

This young man had the right breakthrough in his thinking—he went from thinking about the battles to thinking about the war, from thinking about what was wrong in the small scale of the moment (toothpaste caps, open refrigerator doors) to thinking about what was joyfully right about the lifetime he wanted to share with the woman he loved. He gave up a few battles and won the most important war in his life.

Consider another example from the home front as well, about a mother and her son.

After years of being close with her teenager, a mother found she wasn't spending as much time talking with her son as his schedule got busier and busier. Her long-term goal was an enduring relationship full of warmth, trust, and close communication—she was clear about that. So she planned to go out together for a meal, just one-on-one with her son. She had a nice place in mind, but instead her son wanted to go to Señor Taco, his favorite, loud, bustling hangout. It was hardly the perfect place for close parent/child communication. His mother tried telling him it wasn't a great idea—they wouldn't really be able to talk. By then, though, he was in win-the-battle mode, rolling his eyes and insisting that Señor Taco was the perfect place for a good talk and only a dope wouldn't see that. So the battle was clear: Señor Taco or not Señor Taco.

On the facts, the son was wrong. A quiet restaurant is a better place for a real conversation. But once he was fighting his battle, would any kind of conversation be possible if he lost? And if he were to win, could his mother make a step toward longer-term goals in the process? Without a doubt the answer was yes. Mom let him win, told him, Hey, I'm ready to follow your lead—take me to your Señor Taco. And amid the noise and clamor, they had a long, satisfying talk.

Of course, similar battles happen at work all the time. A skilled worker resists using an important new technology, even though if he'd take the time to master it, he'd see how much easier it would make his job. But he's a staunch defender of his old tools—he feels that to reject the old tools is to reject *him*. Head-to-head, you could force him to abandon the old ways—you *could* win the battle. But the long-term victory here is about building trust and common purpose inside your organization for the long term. Letting the worker win this one—letting him keep his old tools and validating how important they are—is a short-term strategy that builds trust for the long run.

So you let the skilled worker win the battle. For a set period of time he not only keeps his old tools and gets to put off adopting the new technology, but he teaches the values and lessons of the old tools to his colleagues. By letting the skilled worker delay the implementation of the new technology in exchange for his long-term support, you lose the battle but take a step toward winning the war. Let the other guy brag to his friends about how he beat you in a power struggle, so long as next week, or next month, or next year, he's singing off *your* song sheet.

I've consulted with many large companies on technology issues, and I've found that for every firm that fails at a project because they've chosen the wrong technology, three more fail because even though they bet on the right new tools, they didn't plan and communicate well enough with workers at every level. The buzzword here is "readiness." If your company is ready for the big change you're planning, you've got a great chance of making change work. If not, you're doomed.

How do you set the stage for readiness? By building trust over time. By letting the old-timer teach others about his favorite tools. By picking the right moment to let him win a battle, so you can win the war.

Consider another example from the workplace. An organization I once worked with had several divisions, each with a president. One of the presidents went to the parent company's CEO one day and asked flat out, "Why should my group keep sending its profits upstream to you every year instead of reinvesting them in what we do here? What's my motive to keep sending the money up the org chart?" The answer was clear—points to the CEO for honesty—but foolish. "What's your motive?" he responded. "Your paycheck. *You* work for *me*." Needless to say, that division president now works somewhere else. His paycheck was just not enough of a motive for him, and that's true of the most talented people in all industries. Money is an important motivator for them, but not the most important. Pride in their work and dedication to quality are the biggest motives for the very best people in just about all organizations. Otherwise their work could not be as good as it is and they wouldn't be the very best.

The CEO of this large organization won his battle and lost his war. One of his best long-term team players signed off, and that weakened the level of commitment and trust among the other division presidents who stayed behind (as in so many un-balanced companies, the very best people leave, because they have the most options; those who stay behind are generally those who are not as well regarded in their industries).

When you compete in business, the greatest competitive advantage you can have is a carefully thought-out commitment to helping others in the long run. Let the others fight it out to win new business and sell more product for the sake of squeezing more dollars out of the system to buy their new cars and fancier stuff. Your goals should be different. In the long run, business success built on *serving others* helps you accumulate the capital you need to have a lasting positive impact on the world. With the values of service propelling you when you compete, who's going to win? Who's going to build a stronger basis for family life? Who's going to make a real difference to others? Not the competitor who wants to win for the sake of personal rewards, but the man or woman whose power comes from this vital phrase: I can help others. Remember those lines from Alexander Pope:

> *Man, like the generous vine, supported lives;*
> *The strength he gains is from the embrace he gives.*

Focus on the embrace, on giving support to others, and the world will in turn support you. That's the central act of faith that drives success—faith in others, faith in yourself, and faith in the power that comes from sharing your strength.

SAD ICE CREAM: MISSING OUT ON THE JOY

> *Two men ran a wonderful little ice-cream shop—but missed the sweetness and the joy that most people feel when they enter the presence of massive amounts of tasty sweets because they were all too focused on battles they thought they had lost.*

Another lesson about focusing on the war instead of the battles still leaves me shaking my head (and licking my lips) as I think back on it. It revolves around a little ice-cream shop, and the two sad men who worked there.

I was living with my family in a small oceanfront town near Boston when the ice-cream store opened near our house. It was a wonderful shop, a neighborhood place with especially creamy ice cream and lots of creative flavors, like triple-mint mocha and bubblegum explosion. This was in the early 1990s, and the greatest economic boom of the century was just a couple of years away. Within a few years, the Massachusetts economy would bounce particularly high, and the unemployment rate for college graduates with technical skills would close in on zero.

But that was still in the future. The year the ice-cream store opened, the economy was good but not great. Plenty of folks were still a little shaky from the last boom-and-bust cycle, which had included first a spike in real estate prices and then a sharp drop. Many counted the lost equity in their homes as money taken out of their pockets; some who had bought near the top of the market now owed more than their homes were worth. The wheels hadn't quite come off the trolley, but they'd been making some scary noises.

Most people in our town were at the upper end of the income scale. The block I lived on was a little different. It was one of the few streets made up mostly of rentals, though all of the rentals on the block were three-bedroom town houses. That drew an interesting mix of families who needed the space but, for various reasons, didn't want to—or couldn't—buy their own homes. I was there with my own family because I'd just taken a university teaching job, following years in graduate school. It would take a few years to save a down payment. Our neighbors to one side were Russian immigrants, an engineer, a biologist, and their two sons. They were in their forties but had the typical starting-out struggles of newlyweds. Our neighbors to the other side were an all-American family radiating a midwestern optimism. The husband had grown a software company into a substantial business but saw it crash and burn in the economic downturn. After living for a year in a friend's beach house, they'd moved to our little town with their two young children to start over. While his wife spent her time with their kids, the husband took what amounted to an entry-level sales job with another software company and hit the road to build some new accounts and earn his commissions.

Up and down the block, there were similar stories. A midlevel engineer from the General Electric aircraft engine plant, still adjusting to the American workplace from his native England. The one-season pitcher for the Red Sox tending bar and retelling his stories from his year in the big leagues and five years in the minors. The newly divorced young mom and her two sons. The restaurant manager married to a part-time bartender and their two kids. House by house, families were plugging away.

The ice-cream store was a wonderful place for all of us to congregate now and then. Yet it was a bit gloomy as dessert parlors go—mostly because of the owners. A perfectly friendly man in his fifties was there many days. His son, a recent college graduate, worked there, too. Yet both seemed a bit unhappy, and that muted the feelings of indulgence that ice-cream shops naturally encourage.

The father, it turned out, had invested much of his retirement savings in the place. He was an engineer at one of the area manufacturing plants, a twenty-five-year veteran. He didn't particularly want to be moonlighting and seemed tired. So why had he opened the shop? Because his son, who had just finished an undergraduate engineering degree, needed a future. "There's no more jobs like the job I got," he said. No more twenty-five-year gigs, with great benefits and real security. Everything had changed, he said, and he and his son had to scratch some opportunity out of the marketplace, or else the son would have no future at all.

And so father and son worked at their ice-cream shop with little joy, and for all I know they are still at it, making a decent living I'm sure, but still feeling like they deserve more. I imagine them, sad men in one of the world's happier occupations, bending over their barrels of ice cream with bitter feelings, as the great economic boom of the late 1990s unfolds outside their doors, tripling real estate prices, driving salaries up and up and up, and creating waves of new opportunities. Perhaps they shut down the ice-cream shop and started a Web-based business of some sort as they took stock of the new boom. Perhaps the son walked away and put his engineering degree to more conventional use as local tech firms chased after new tech grads with a vengeance. Perhaps they made some real money and saved it. Perhaps they bet on a dot-com and won big, maybe holding on to their gains, or riding the coaster up and back down.

Whatever happened to these decent, hardworking men, I continue to think of them as victims of their own pessimism, and as classic win-the-battle types. There was the father, declaring to all that the good days were largely over, and that only grudging enterprise could keep a young man's prospects alive. There was the son, not sure what to think, gloomy about the future but perhaps hoping for a happy surprise. And there were the rest of my neighbors, on the prowl for opportunity, placing new bets on the future day in and day out, and making their own good luck with each passing hour.

You could have found plenty of evidence to support the pessimism of the ice-cream man. And you could have convinced my neighbors that their pasts were the best predictors of their futures, their own optimism nothing but illusion. Another bankruptcy will surely follow for the man who lost his software company. The Russian immigrants would find new barriers, new bosses and bullies who pulled the strings in our society. But the optimists would be the winners in the long run. The faith in opportunity and the courage to accept struggle and even failure, and then to keep at the enterprise of building your own success, were proven to be the best path. And that will always be so.

My neighbors were, for the most part, fighting the war. They were working their jobs, making their plans, enjoying their families, and rolling their eyes with deep pleasure as they licked their ice-cream cones. They had good luck and bad, but not one of them ever focused with such determination on bad luck or missed opportunity that ice cream would taste bad. I'm afraid the ice-cream shop owners were so focused on the lost battle—the fact that the year the son graduated from engineering school there were no good engineering jobs for him—they were giving up on the war. The son was going into ice cream instead of engineering—by no means a terrible fate—with a heavy heart, feeling like a victim, refusing to let go of that lost battle. And so, clinging to that lost battle, the two men at the ice-cream shop on the corner presided over the saddest sweet shop I've ever been to.

A Lesson from Augustine: Fight *for* What You Love, Not *Against* What You Hate

Fighting against what you don't like is less important and less productive than fighting for what you do like. Making more of what's good is more virtuous and more productive than trying to eliminate what's bad.

Augustine of Hippo—known to many as Saint Augustine—was a North African philosopher in the years following the adoption of Christianity as the official church of the late Roman Empire. Augustine lived in a time when there were many opportunities to study different, and often clashing, versions of Christian philosophy. In his book *Confessions*, Augustine talks about his experience studying with a group called the Manicheans, who had a stark view of the difference between good and evil. They believed that evil was an active force, always looking for chances to triumph over good.

Eventually, Augustine broke away from them and created his own vision of the difference between good and evil—evil, he proposed, was simply the absence of good. Augustine saw that evil was not an active force constantly looking for victory over good, but instead was a passive thing, an absence of goodness.

Instead of constantly trying to fight evil, as the Manicheans did, and seeking to win every battle, Augustine proposed that we ought to spend more time thinking about the nature of goodness and focusing on the larger issues of grace and virtue. We'll win the fight against evil not by beating it back every hour of every day, but by winning the far more important war to be better people ourselves, to create more of what's good rather than trying to eliminate the things we think are bad. The good we create will drive the bad out without our having to play the negative roles of warriors *against* evil. We have the greater privilege of being *for* something better, instead.

Thus Augustine is in some ways the founder of the "focus on the war, not the battle" philosophy, way back around the year 400. His lesson that we need to be for what we believe in, rather than against our enemies, is one of the greatest insights in human history. If you have a hard relationship with a spouse, a child, a parent, or a coworker, focus on what you're for in your relationship, the good things you want more of, and build on them, rather than focusing on the bad and trying to drive it out. If you look at yourself and see some failings, focus on what you actually like about yourself, about what you do right, and make that part of you stronger, instead of trying to beat down the dark side. If you want to help solve a problem in your community, look for what's working and put your shoulder into making more of that, rather than taking up the cudgels to fight head on against the bad stuff. You can fight what's wrong by falling more in love with what's right—that's the positive path to success.

Two Lessons from St. Augustine

Evil is not an active force, but simply the absence of goodness. So to fight evil, focus on making more goodness, not on winning battles against the bad.

Put more goodness in the world, and a corresponding amount of evil will disappear, without having to win any battles against it.

Clarify Your Goals

You can't focus on the war instead of the battle until you are crystal clear about what the war is—what your personal long-term goals are. Figure out the game you are playing—figure out where you plan to be when you reach your goals—and that clarity will become the foundation of your success.

Many people focus on battles because they don't think long term at all—they don't focus on the war because they're not living their lives in terms of long-term goals. That's a trap you can beat. You *can* take the high ground—you can fight and win the war while others are focused on the battles—but only *if* you know the nature of the war that you are fighting.

The good news is that it's up to you. Even though most people don't put a lot of thought into their long-term goals—and therefore wind up fighting other people's wars and playing other people's games—you can fight your own war and play your own game. You *can* create that context for your day-to-day and week-to-week struggles in a way that gives them even greater meaning and purpose than you might be able to imagine.

It goes back to that one powerful personal statement: "I can help."

You get to decide how you will help others. Perhaps by becoming wealthy, and then using your money to help people you care about become healthy, educated, and independent. Or perhaps by devoting time to teaching young people things they need to know, or ways of reaching their own goals. Or perhaps by capturing images of how people live in far-flung places, to bring an understanding of those people into your own community. Whatever path you choose, so long as your long-term goal is a goal of service, a goal of helping others, you are exercising the power to succeed. You can let others win the battles. Simply by being mindful of the difference between short-term struggles and long-term goals, you gain an edge in how you think and feel and act. You see more and know more than you would if you were totally stuck in the moment.

One of the best examples of seeing the difference between long-term and short-term goals comes from a teacher named James Herndon. Herndon was one of the world's greatest average teachers, and I think he'd enjoy having that description applied to him. He wrote a handful of books about his life in the classroom, always humble in their telling, never making himself a hero, and confessing to as much failure as success in working with inner-city California middle-school students. He never seemed above the fray. He was in the fight to make it through the day just as much as he was in the intellectual game of *thinking* about school and education.

Herndon celebrates the brilliance of his students as well as their limitations and bad habits. He also celebrates his own limitations. The careful reader eventually catches on that each failure for Herndon, each victory of the students over his attempts to teach them something, is a finer moment of education than whatever the subverted lesson plan might have called for. Consider, for example, this tiny story:

> "Where do you live, Mr. Herndon?" kids ask every day. "See that tower?" I ask. Everyone abandons work to take a look at the tower. I fall for it every time. "*That's* where I live!" Quite a few kids then fall to arguing about whether I really live in, on, or about that tower.

In point of fact, Herndon lived *near* the tower, in a little house with his family. Like so many of us, he enjoyed looking out the window and saying "I live there," connecting his home and his work, offering evidence that he had a broader life than his work in school. So, yes, he was falling for it, tricked into giving the faintest excuse for his students to stop looking down at their desks and start looking up and out the window at the world. And clearly he was happy to let their minds wander a bit, to point up and out to the physical world they share and think about *that* for a while.

But he also loved talking about that question—Where do you live?—because of the subtler questions hidden within it: What do you care about? What are your values? What kind of person are you? He answered these questions in the very act of letting his students fool him. He was the kind of teacher who enjoyed seeing students leap from their seats, animated and alive. He cared about the connections he made with them, about being real, being three-dimensional, a man with a job and a home, with a mind and a heart. He was the kind of teacher ready to subvert his own planned lesson now and then, hoping for an enlightening surprise, hoping for some bigger lesson to come from his students than could possibly come from his plans. Now and then, these hopes were rewarded, as they are (now and then) for the rest of us.

Herndon could have fought harder to win the battles against his students—as far too many teachers do—but then he would have taught them larger lessons about discipline and order that were entirely the opposite of what he truly believed, and truly wanted to communicate to his youngsters. "I fall for it every time," he confesses, knowing that he'd been beaten in his battles, but had won a much more important war. He savored his larger victory, the warmth and the human touch that filled his classroom. That's the real lesson and legacy of James Herndon: a lesson in overcoming the structures and barriers—like the difference between students and teachers, like rigid lesson plans and curriculum goals—that keep us apart.

6

KNOWING THE REAL THING WHEN YOU SEE IT

THE ART OF REFRAMING THE GAME

It's a lot easier to focus on the right goals when your personal life is doing just fine and work is going well. But how can you find the right focus when things are plain rotten? The best answer—and an answer that works in just about all cases—is that when you find yourself losing, it's time to pay more attention to your fundamental beliefs and long-term goals—it's time to play a bigger game.

Of course, it's easy to be insightful when you are winning. Ask the new college graduate how she made it through school, and she'll probably have lots of useful advice. Ask the business owner who just cashed out for big money what strategies she used and she'll probably be ready to talk for hours.

But what about when you're on the losing side of the game? When you're out of work, when you feel relationships heading in the wrong direction, when you see your kids going off the track? How can you find insight when you need it most?

The best answer—and an answer that works in just about all cases—is that when you find yourself losing, it's time to play a bigger game. It's also useful to think about this as "reframing" the game. A couple of examples can help make this clear.

Radio talk-show host Bruce Williams now reaches millions of people every day on the air. Before he turned to radio, though, he was a notable citizen in his New Jersey town. He owned businesses and had been involved in local politics for years, even serving a term as mayor. In the mid-1970s, he ran for Congress and lost—a dispiriting experience. Now, though, he realizes that losing the election was the best thing that could have happened to him. Not long after, he started his radio career, something he could not have done as a congressman. I don't know Williams but I enjoy his show, and I do believe that his motives in running for office were more about having the chance to do good things for his potential constituents than personal gain. I also think that his radio show reflects his own values—it's a personal show, full of advice that reflects Williams's experience and beliefs.

Politicians are notoriously self-involved, and they tend to take their victories and losses personally. (Winston Churchill, after his party's dramatic losses shortly after World War II—losses that effectively bounced Churchill out of the prime ministry—was told by a friend, "Winston, this is a blessing in disguise." His response: "In that case, the disguise is perfect.") So I know it must have been hard for Williams to see the war instead of the battle. But look at what this lost battle enabled him to do—build an outlet to reach and serve millions of people every day. The thousands he would have represented in Congress might miss out, but the millions who benefit from his life on the radio get the benefit. Because Williams is now engaged in the bigger project of helping as many people as he can, we can see his tactical loss as a great strategic victory. And he seems to agree. On his website, he explains that for years he made contributions to the guy who beat him, a small way of saying thank you.

The story of Martin Luther King's leadership of the Montgomery bus boycott in 1955 and 1956 offers another, profound example of reframing the game. King was a member of the elite of southern African American society, tremendously well educated and always on the right side of the law. During the bus boycott, he and the others in the movement were harassed by the police in Montgomery regularly. Their movements were monitored, they were arrested for petty traffic infractions, they were denied permits to hold peaceful protests. All along in the early months of the movement, King and the leadership worked desperately hard to avoid going to jail, in great part because they wanted their movement to be respectable. For an African American man in the Deep South to go to jail meant, especially for King, crossing a powerful social line. It meant losing respectability. It meant conforming to the ugly stereotypes of being dangerous. And it meant losing the ability to sit with white leaders in the community and negotiate for positive change. But as the months went by, King's efforts to keep the movement in motion without going jail were failing, and he was deeply troubled. Finally, he came to the conclusion that he would have to go to jail—that the battle to stay free of that social stain was beginning to take a toll on his ability to win the war for justice that he was fighting.

When the day finally came, he was picked up on a fabricated speeding charge, separated from his colleagues, put in the back of a police cruiser, and driven off, away from the jail. Where were they taking him? As they drove under an unfamiliar bridge, King "was sure now that I was going to meet my fateful hour on the other side." But the jail suddenly loomed ahead—the police were toying with King, driving him in circles for a while to make him sweat. As he was led into a holding cell, "gusts of emotion swept through me like cold winds on an open prairie. For the first time in my life I had been thrown behind bars."

And what did he find there? He found the future. He found that jail made him stronger, and that yielding to the bogus charges, actually trying to *fill* the jails when the movement organized protests, gave the civil rights movement greater passion, more national and international visibility, and the clear moral high ground. Fighting to keep out of jail turned out to be a battle worth losing. The bigger war, the war for social justice for African American people, was helped immeasurably by that lost battle. "From that night on," King later wrote about his first night in jail, "my commitment to the struggle for freedom was stronger than ever before."

Knowing the Real Thing When You See It

KNOW WHEN YOU'VE LOST, AND TURN A BATTLE INTO A WAR

> *This is a story about how I lost a job I really wanted—and why that turned out to be the best thing that could have happened to me. The battle I lost turned out to mean little once I focused on my larger goals and found other—in the long run, better—ways to reach them. I was able to reframe the game, and play it at a higher level.*

Sales consultant Rick Page has written about the advice he gives high-level salespeople who waste their time and money pursuing deals that they've already blown. He tells them, "You took a bullet a while ago, you just didn't know when to die and fall down." Bruce Williams had the insight to die as a politician and return to life as a radio host.

I had my own moment of the undead when I was in my twenties and up for a big job at a midwestern college, running a program called Leadership, Ethics and Values, which combined in one package all of my passions as a scholar and teacher. I went out to spend a week at the college after I made the list of three finalists for the position. A good friend was already teaching there and gave me a solid sense of how the place worked—and it was all good news as far as I was concerned. During that week, I gave lectures, taught classes, and got to know dozens of professors and scores of students. After my last day on campus, as I was packing up in my hotel room, my friend on the faculty called with some unofficial news. "I didn't want to tell you earlier," he said, "because I didn't want any of this to affect your performance this week, but now that it's over you should know that the first candidate for the job was here last week and nobody liked him." That sounded like a good thing for my own chances. "You're the second candidate, and you made a great impression." Even better. "The third candidate, who was supposed to come visit next week, called a couple of days ago and withdrew from the search." Excellent.

My friend called me the next day at home. "More news," he said. "The selection committee for the job met and they chose you." Awesome! I began to think about where in town my family would be buying our new house. Right near the college? Closer to the old stone train station? Good choices, both. . . . All that remained, my friend told me, was for the president to sign off on the selection committee's recommendation, and I'd have an official offer in my hands in a few days. Sounded great to me.

But the president never did sign off, and I was hugely disappointed when I learned that he had decided that no one at all would get the job. He had apparently been hoping for someone with more of a national reputation to take it over, someone older. Failing that, he was prepared to let Leadership, Ethics and Values move to the back burner with a fill-in director and diminishing financial support.

I'd never had a clue what the president was looking for—I was totally focused instead on what the search committee and the professors I met on campus told me. But the president was the real decision maker and he had his own ideas. I had not even begun to fight for the president's approval because I was focused on winning the battle for the selection committee's nod. A friend who held a senior sales job at a big mutual fund company heard my story and told me "Man, you made a classic selling mistake—you sold to the wrong level." He was certainly

right, but there was more to it. His answer was about tactics—
a better salesman with better tactics might have gotten the job.
But getting the job was only a short-term, battle-level goal. I
just didn't realize that at the time.

I sat in my apartment in a daze. As the process unfolded, I
had become more and more certain of getting the job. I was already congratulating myself, already thinking of myself as a
winner. So without the job, what was I? For a while, it was hard
for me to answer that question. Once the game was over, I had
trouble paying attention to my family. I couldn't read a book. I
couldn't concentrate. I was depressed, and it took time to lift.

And, of course, not getting that job turned out to be the best
thing that possibly could have happened. I had been paying attention to the battle—getting the job directing the program in
Leadership, Ethics and Values at a small midwestern college,
where I might have been able to reach one or two thousand college students in the classroom, and a few hundred scholars and
professors with my research and other writing. But after losing
the job—losing the battle—I refocused on the war. I reframed
the game by looking at what my long-term goals really were—
reaching people with important ideas about leadership, ideas
about ethics, and ideas about values. Ironically, a few years later
my family and I did wind up moving to that very same midwestern town, though we were looking at real estate a couple of
rungs up the ladder from what a new professor might be able
to buy. We were moving to town because I had a new job as
president of the Great Books Foundation, a fifty-year-old organization reaching thirty thousand adults and over a million students with programs in literature, ethics, and civic leadership. I
was making about four times the salary of the college job, had a
staff of about seventy, and got to serve many more people than

I'd ever have been able to as director of the Leadership, Ethics and Values program.

My failure was good for me. The battle I lost turned out to mean little once I focused on my larger goals and found other—in the long run, better—ways to reach them. I was able to reframe the game and play it at a higher level.

Part of my problem in the heat of the battle for the college job was pride. I wanted to be a winner. Had I fought harder for that job, applied again the following year, kept in touch with the president and worked to meet his vision of the position, maybe I could have eventually won the battle—and lost the chance to do bigger things at the Great Books Foundation. That would have been pure level-one thinking driven by the desire to see myself as a winner.

Level-two thinking might have helped me focus on looking more impressive to the president—a tactical advantage, but still more attuned to the battle, not the war.

Level-three thinking led to the better challenge and turned a failure into a small part of a larger victory. Level-three thinking presented me with the right challenge; it led me to ask, How can I help more people meet *their* own goals? That question took me out of the academy, focused me on helping my own family meet its goals (earning enough to buy a nice house was one of those goals), and, eventually, helped me play a role in serving more than a million people.

KNOWING THE REAL THING WHEN YOU SEE IT

> *Will you know the real thing when you see it? The right person to share your life with, the perfect job, the risk*

HOW TO KNOW WHEN YOU'VE LOST A BATTLE, AND IT'S TIME TO
REFRAME THE GAME:

You realize you've been focusing on level 1 or level 2, not level 3.

You hear the needs of the people you are trying to help and you
have to admit that you can't help with those needs.

You know you *can* help but you realize you've lost the credibility
and trust needed to be an effective helper.

HOW TO RESPOND:

Reframe the game in terms of long-term goals to help others.

If you can't help the people you set out to help, help others.

Use failure as an opportunity to strengthen and increase your
ambition.

Focus on trust—if it's absent, build it by helping others reach
their goals.

---

*that's truly worth taking? Developing the insight to tell
the real thing from the run-of-the-mill involves knowing
who you are yourself, and knowing what you believe in.*

A good friend of mine has been very successful in his business
life. He earned the chance to break off from the large publishing company he helped grow from $50 million a year in sales to
$500 million and set up his own company in his garage. That
gave him more time—and closer proximity—to be with his
four children. In some ways he's still a kid himself (his personal
collection of go-karts now fills part of the garage his business
outgrew a couple of years ago). But he's also a traditional father

with a strong desire to help his children find their way in the world. One question he likes to ask them is, "Would you know the real thing if you saw it?"

That question points in a lot of different directions. When you have a problem and you're looking for an answer, will you know the *best* answer when you see it? Will you be able to tell the bad solutions from the good? When you're looking for a friend—or a boyfriend, a spouse, a teacher, or a business partner—will you be able to tell the person truly capable of caring about you from the others?

But there's more to this question—would you know the real thing if you saw it?—than practical issues. It's also the question at the very heart of Christianity. Would you know God if he walked among us as a poor carpenter? It's an important question for Judaism, for Greek mythology, for Islam, and for a host of other religions as well. In fact, the theme of the hidden prophet seems to be as old as humanity—wise men and women seem to have always understood that the answers to our questions (and perhaps the answers to our prayers) are often sitting close at hand, waiting for us to develop the skill to see them for what they are.

A follower of Judaism in the time of the biblical prophets might have had the clarity of mind and soul to recognize the prophet Elijah disguised as a beggar. A citizen of ancient Jerusalem might have seen in the carpenter from Nazareth divinity itself.

That is the task of developing insight—learning to know the real thing when it stands before you. In the Christian bible, Jesus walks among men *as a man,* without thunderbolts or attending angels to give everyone else the signal, *Hey! Here's the Messiah! Pay attention to what he's saying!* Instead, it is up to thinking individuals to demonstrate their own insight—to see past the cloak of the ordinary and to find the spark of divinity that lies not only within Elijah and Jesus, but within every man and woman, every prince and every beggar.

One of the most creative thinkers I've ever met is a scientist named Kary Mullis. He won the Nobel Prize for Chemistry in 1993 for inventing a way to make millions of identical copies of individual strands of DNA. Without this remarkable invention, most of the things we do with DNA today, including DNA finger-printing in crime investigations and many of the medical applications of DNA science, would be impossible. Millions of people owe Kary Mullis thanks for making their lives better, and longer, than they'd otherwise be.

Mullis had his brainstorm about the process for replicating DNA while driving his car north on a California highway. His girlfriend, also a PhD chemist, was in the car with him, dozing while they tooled up the highway to their weekend cottage. As the pieces of the puzzle fell into place, he pulled off the high-way, knowing that he'd had a monster breakthrough idea. He woke her up. "I told her something incredible had just occurred to me." And now, twenty years later, we know that what Mullis was experiencing was the real thing—a world-changing idea. How did this young chemist in the car beside him react? "She yawned and leaned against the window to go back to sleep." She missed the real thing.

In the cabin, Mullis spins his ideas back and forth. He writes chemical equations on the walls. His mind goes nonstop. His girl-friend doesn't buy it; she's bored by his excitement after a couple of hours. Back in his office the following Monday, he searches the scientific literature—no one else has proposed anything like this, and no obvious obstacles to pulling it off are on the horizon. He starts talking up the idea with his scientific colleagues.

"However," he later wrote, "shocking to me, not one of my friends or colleagues would get excited over the potential for such a process. True, I was always having wild ideas, and this one maybe looked no different from last week's. But it *was* different." In the long run, Mullis was proven right. His employer at the time eventually sold the rights to the process for $300 million—and even at that price, the buyer got a bargain. Mullis became something of a celebrity and wound up with a wonderful platform for his unceasing flow of wild—and sometimes correct—new ideas. As he likes to say, with a Nobel Prize, you can open any door, at least once.

But why did so many people fail to grasp how big his idea was? Why didn't they see that Mullis had reached a breakthrough that would change everything in the way DNA science worked? The very question holds the answer—most people don't want to see everything change. They don't want to have the comfortable world they have built rocked to its core. And they don't want to buy in to an idea that other people will find nutty for exactly those same reasons. It's all classic second-level thinking. Someone shows you the way to turn dirt into gold—and it really works. But you know that anyone who stands up and says "Hey, I can turn dirt into gold" will be laughed at, even if it turns out to be true. Most people are all too good at imagining how they will look to others if they break the mold and start talking about radical ideas—even radical ideas that are true and important. It takes a courageous man like Mullis to think more about what his new process will be able to do to help other people than about how he'll be treated when he starts talking about another wild new idea. Mullis saw his idea as a part of the larger human story of science, enriching everyone. The fact that a radical new idea might complicate his own small story, and how other people viewed him, meant little, because he was a true believer in the value of science for humankind. When the real thing peeked its head up, he could not help pointing and stomping his feet and whooping and hollering, no matter how silly he might look to others.

LESSONS FROM HANNAH ARENDT: THINKING CRITICALLY ABOUT YOURSELF

> *Thinking critically about who you are, what you believe,
> and when you are prepared to say no to authority in
> order to preserve your values is an essential trait for personal integrity, for helping others, and for ensuring your
> own success.*

Here's an example of recognizing the real thing—but in reverse. It's about being able to recognize the worst qualities in ourselves, instead of the best. The twentieth-century philosopher Hannah Arendt was a refugee from Nazism when she arrived in the United States during World War II. She was a remarkably well-educated woman, with a PhD from a German university and a razor-sharp mind. Arendt had been close to the German philosopher Karl Jaspers, who resisted Nazism throughout World War II, though she also had a romantic interlude with philosopher Martin Heidegger, who was a collaborator. She managed to get out of Germany and into France at the war's start, though as a German citizen she was sent to an internment camp in southern France. She had two strikes against her in France—she was a German national, which made her an enemy of the French state in those years before France fell to the German army, and she was Jewish, which roused the anti-Semitism in the French leadership at the time. Arendt, ever resourceful, was able to escape from the French internment camp and made her way to America, where she worked first as a housekeeper, then as an aid worker, a teacher, and a writer. Though English was her fifth language, her best-known work was written in that adopted language.

Twenty years after arriving in the United States, Arendt was sent to Israel by the *New Yorker* magazine to cover the trial of Nazi functionary Adolph Eichmann, who had been responsible for the deportation and deaths of more than a million Jews from Eastern Europe. Even as Russian and American troops were closing in on Hungary and the victory over the Nazis was clear for all to see, Eichmann worked with cruel efficiency to keep trainloads of Jewish Hungarians—tens of thousands of men, women, and children—streaming to the death camps in the final weeks of the war.

After the war, Eichmann, like many Nazi leaders, slipped out of Germany and built a new life for himself in Argentina. In 1960, Israeli secret agents found him, smuggled him out of South America and into Israel, and put him on trial for crimes against humanity.

Arendt coined the term "the banality of evil" to describe the way Eichmann became a mass murderer—not by following any passionate hatred, but only by going along with his peers and following the orders of authorities. He did evil, Arendt tells us, not because he was deeply bad in some absolute sense, but because he did not have the habit of thinking critically about what other people did and wanted him to do. About Eichmann she wrote, "There was no sign in him of firm ideological convictions or of specific evil motives, and the only notable characteristic one could detect in his past behavior as well as in his behavior during the trial . . . was something entirely negative: it was not stupidity but *thoughtlessness*." Eichmann's moral failure—in a sense, the ultimate moral failure—was the product not of the active presence of evil, but of the lack of reflective thought, and, following that, the lack of insight. He did not seek to understand what he was doing, to connect the work at hand to its larger meaning. He simply did as he was told.

As Arendt described him, Eichmann was unobjectionable—a cog in the machine, an organization man. Given how monstrous his actions were, though, it is fair to ask, would we know a man capable of such horror if we saw such a man?

Here's another way to ask the same question, with a similar historical setting. Public schoolteachers in Nazi Germany were, of course, government employees. As Nazi ideology took over the state, all government employees were ordered to wear swastikas over their work clothes every day. Some teachers did not and were fired (some killed). Others—most—simply put their swastikas on and kept about their work. Here's the test of whether you would know the real thing if you saw it: who among the teachers *you've* had would have refused to wear the symbol of Nazism under those conditions? Who would have had that courage and integrity? If you can develop that degree of insight, you can reach your goals without a doubt.

THIRD-LEVEL QUESTIONS FOR THE REAL THING

What questions would we ask if we were in the presence of someone who was the real thing? The question that Socrates asked often might be the best one: what does the truly good life look like? Questions like this, connecting

*our values with our action, do more than help us reach
our practical goals; they help us deserve the success we
fight for and win. They help us be more than strong.
They help us be good.*

Three Lessons from Hannah Arendt

People do terrible things more often out of the urge to
conform—because they are worried about how others
perceive them—than from a desire to do harm.

Reflective thought and real insight are necessary for moral behavior.

Helping other people to think critically helps them be more
moral, and more successful in the long run.

What happens when you ask third-level questions of a man or
woman who *is* the real thing—someone with a mission to make
the world a better place? Here is Odysseus disguised as an old
beggar as he visits his son in Homer's Greek epic *The Odyssey*.
How does he see himself? What are his goals? He wants to see
how the people of his kingdom live when their king is absent.
He wants to look into their hearts and see how good they are to
one another, and how dedicated to a spirit of community they
remain, when the source of authority in their kingdom isn't there.
In short, he wants to better understand the people he leads.

Ask the same questions of Elijah, who appeared at the gates
of a small town in biblical times, as a beggar dying of thirst, and
the answer will be, he wished to challenge ordinary people to
take the risk of helping others. A single mother took in Elijah,

the starving beggar, fed him, and put a roof over his head. That was a risk for this woman, but she put her faith in humanity above her natural fear. When her young son became tragically ill shortly after, Elijah brought him back from the dead, one of the great miracles of the Hebrew bible.

Ask the questions to Jesus, and what will you hear? There are many ways to answer that question. Why did Jesus live among ordinary men and women? What did he understand as his mission and his goals? My personal answer is this: to bring divinity face-to-face with man, in order to inspire men and women to reach the heights of decency they were built to attain, but which they often lost sight of among the petty struggles and pleasures of life.

The lessons of these prophets are deep and complex. They include my friend's question—Will you know the real thing when you see it?—and other questions, too, including these: Will we recognize our own potential for decency and for greatness and live up to that potential? Will we see the real thing within ourselves and fulfill our own potential to be decent, caring members of the human community?

As we dedicate ourselves to meeting the practical goals in our lives—family goals, financial goals, goals about material things—these bigger questions are incredibly important. They do even more than help us reach our practical goals; they help us deserve the success we fight for and win. They help us be more than strong. They help us be good. They give us the power of purpose.

Aristotle's insistence on active virtue—virtuous *action*—over passive virtue speaks directly to the challenge we all face of being as good as we have the potential to be. Any one of us can sit around and think virtuous thoughts, but to stand up and act out virtuous actions is another thing entirely. But that's what Aristotle tells us—for every good thought we think, we need to add a good action. For every feeling of sympathy we feel, we ought to add some active expression of our feelings. We have to walk the talk. Otherwise we will allow our societies to be led by those who might not share our values, but have greater inclination to stand up and get things done. As the British philosopher Edmund Burke famously said, "All that is necessary for evil to triumph is for good men to do nothing."

REAL PROBLEMS

> *How can you tell the difference between a problem that needs more energy and time to get fixed, and a lost cause that you need to write off and move past? The key is in asking the right questions, and discovering which challenges represent the real hopes and dreams of the people you care about—these are the problems you need to stick with.*

Knowing when to admit failure is essential to reaching our goals. If you can't figure out the difference between a lost cause and an obstacle you can overcome by hitting it a little harder, you'll spend too much time banging into immovable objects, and too little pushing against the walls that are ready to fall. You'll also miss the chance to prevent bigger problems from growing out of smaller ones.

Think back to sales consultant Rick Page and his observation that salespeople sometimes lose sales because they don't realize that they've already failed ("you took a bullet a while ago, you just didn't know when to die and fall down"). By staying on her feet and continuing to plug away at Sales Opportunity A, a sales professional fails to go out and win Sales Opportunity B—that's left for the competition, whose job is now easier, competing against an undead competitor miles away in another (and hopeless) prospect's office.

Here's the fundamental challenge: Will you recognize and learn from real failure as well as success? Will you be able to reframe your game, so you'll use the lessons from Sales Opportunity A to infuse time, energy, and insight into Sale B?

Here's another example. You've been struggling all year with your teenage son to keep his room clean. Sometimes he gets it, sometimes he doesn't, and the socks in the hallway near his room, the pile of smelly clothes heaped on the unmade bed— it just drives you crazy. He's a good talker and admits he's not doing he best he can do, but he just doesn't come through consistently. But then he starts getting better—he starts making the bed every day, and there's much less mess in his room. Sure, he's out more often with school activities, but when he's home, he's less of a problem, even though he's got less time to talk. Would you know a real problem with this boy if you saw it? You're seeing it now. A sudden improvement in behavior coupled with less talk and less time at home is a danger sign—the child might be making progress, but just as likely he's now following more surface rules in order to mask a deeper problem. This is a level-two response—he's tuning into how you see him—but if he's not also spending time talking with you, that avoidance is a big clue that his interest in how you see him stems from something he's hiding. It's defensive behavior because he has a secret.

How can you develop your insight to be able to spot potential problems like this one? Focus on the three levels of thought, and work on asking level-three questions to yourself and to others as often as possible. Your greatest insight as a parent will come when you focus less on the explicit behavior of your children and more on their wishes, dreams, and goals. That doesn't mean you loosen the rules of behavior. But it does mean that you focus those rules more on the long run than the short run—more on building strong habits and respect for others than on looking good and being inoffensive in the short run. It means asking, as often as you can, what your children are dreaming of, wishing for, and thinking about.

And the same questions will do wonders for your relationships with your friends, your colleagues, your customers, and your neighbors.

I had an experience when I was a teenager that illustrates this challenge well. I was working at a summer camp for children with physical handicaps. The children were a sweet group of kids, most in my group about eleven years old. Many used wheelchairs; a few lived with shortened limbs and pretty severe physical disabilities. The work was meaningful, but very difficult at first. After a few days of playing and working with the kids, I felt drained. In fact, I felt like I couldn't handle the work anymore. I sat in my bunk and cried and decided that I had to leave because I just wasn't strong enough emotionally for this work.

The head of the camp was away for a day, and I went in to see the assistant head. She was kind to me, said she understood, but asked me to wait one day until the head came back so that he and I could make the proper arrangements for my departure. I went back to my bunk feeling relieved, but also very disappointed in myself. Still, I felt I didn't have the resources to keep going.

The next morning, I sat with the director, and he said something that really touched me. He said that he was very sorry to see me leave. "I've watched you with the kids," he said, "and I've seen real love in you for them. You can do this. You should think about staying." I didn't expect him to say anything like that, and it blew me over. I didn't realize how much I needed to hear that praise, how the resources that had been drained by the emotional demands of that job could be built back up with some honest praise and personal support. The camp director was teaching me a very important lesson. I thought I had failed at the larger task of working at the camp. In fact, I had failed at the smaller task of finding some balance and emotional nourishment. He could tell the difference. By helping me admit and overcome that smaller failure, he gave me the strength to succeed at the larger, and much more important, task.

7

THE POWER OF PURPOSE

BE AT THE CENTER AND AT THE FRINGE

Find your greatest power by balancing the wild with the tame, the calm with the passionate, the new big idea with time-tested wisdom.

Most of us fall into one of two categories—we're either more comfortable at the center of things, or more comfortable on the fringe. We tend to prefer having the comfort and safety of being in the mainstream—working for established companies, in established industries; following social expectations and not seeming like a bunch of oddballs—or being on the cutting edge—working as entrepreneurs, pioneering new business models, bucking convention and standing out in the crowd as being a bit different. But the smartest and most successful people understand that wherever they fit naturally, either at the center or the fringe, looking to the *other extreme* for inspiration and strength—the opposite of what comes naturally for you— creates tremendous advantages. That is to say, if you're some- one more comfortable at the center, you need the creativity of the fringe to supercharge your life. If you're more comfortable at the fringe, you need the stability of the center to balance yourself and make your creativity usable for ordinary people. The challenge is to be at the center AND the fringe at the same time—to think from two different perspectives at once.

CASE STUDY: THE RISE OF THE INTERNET

> *The greatest advance of our age grew from the combined efforts of a billion-dollar federal research project staffed by PhDs, and a roomful of college kids fueled by Pop- Tarts and Jolt Cola.*

The rise of the Internet is one of the great examples of balanc- ing the center and the fringe to create world-altering results. The Internet began its life as a massive, billion-dollar project of the U.S. Defense Department. In fact, the network of comput- ers that we now call the Internet was called DARPAnet for sev- eral years first—standing for the Defense Advanced Research Projects Agency network. The money came from taxes paid by millions of Americans; it was authorized by Congress and over- seen by layers of bureaucracy, military brass, and legislative fact finders. There could hardly be a more "center"-driven project.

And it could not have worked otherwise—it just took too much money and required too much cooperation from inherently conservative government research facilities, major universities, and the military.

I was a user of the early Internet, and I can tell you it looked nothing like what we find online today. First, it was ugly. There were no images—just text, and little attention paid to making the system easy to use. Also, it was filled with technical information and had little to offer people outside of universities and government labs. There were no such things as Web browsers or multimedia interactivity. Instead the Internet provided access to plain-vanilla text-only e-mail and text-only research services with names like Gopher and Veronica, hosted mostly by research labs and big universities.

But then something amazing happened. I remember a friend telling me I should download the new Internet tool called Mosaic, that it could totally change the way the Internet looked. I called the technical support people at Harvard, where I worked at the time, and they told me their systems couldn't support Mosaic, but that changed in a hurry. Mosaic became the killer application of the early Internet, and within a couple of years it morphed into Netscape and the commercial, fun-to-use Internet was born.

But Mosaic wasn't invented by the government, didn't take thousands or hundreds or even dozens of researchers to invent, and was about as "fringe" as you could get. Led by a student named Marc Andreessen, a small team of University of Illinois dorm dwellers wrote the code for Mosaic over a few months, sleeping on the university computer center floors and fueling their work with Pop-Tarts and Jolt cola.

Without the billions of dollars and the massive institutional support of DARPA, the Internet could not have been built. But without the sleepless, smelly, overcaffeinated students on the computer center floor out in Champaign, Illinois, the work of DARPA would fall more in the category of awesome government science projects—perhaps like NASA or the Superconducting SuperCollider—than in the category of pervasive cultural tools like radio or television, where it sits today. It was the combination of both—of the center and the fringe—that made the magic that, in turn, built the Internet.

The modern jet airplane is another case in point, the product of a business that found a way to be at the center and at the fringe at the same time. In 1943, the Lockheed Aircraft Corporation, already a large war contractor at that point, allowed a very small group of workers to form what they called their SkunkWorks, an intense, entrepreneurial corps that had the mission to reinvent air travel, free of Lockheed bureaucracy, budget oversight, and old institutional habits. In 143 days, they invented the P-30 "Shooting Star" jet fighter plane, the first functional jet aircraft.

The modern computer desktop is the result of a similar SkunkWorks project, when Apple Computer founder Steve Jobs headed up a renegade research and development project to craft what became the Apple Macintosh, the first commercial computer to use a mouse and allow users to click on images instead of typing commands or choosing selections from long text lists of options. Though Apple Computer was already a great success at the time, Jobs knew that the company needed to take a quantum leap ahead in the marketplace or it would die. John Scully, the Apple CEO Jobs had recruited, didn't share his vision. Scully was a classic "center" thinker, formerly a top executive at Pepsi. So Jobs took a handful of employees, invaded an Apple building on the edge of the Apple Computer corporate campus, and worked in isolation with his team to reinvent the personal computer. Over their building, Jobs flew a pirate flag.

Jobs and his team were on the fringe, literally. They were isolated within Apple, but they were still on the team. Jobs could have simply started a new company to develop his vision. But he didn't. He stuck with Apple as an internal dissident rather than leaving as a deserter. Working alone, without the power and wisdom that Scully and the rest of the Apple infrastructure represented to balance his own wild insights and tremendous will to succeed, Jobs likely would not have succeeded. In fact, his next project—called, of all things, NEXT—flopped, in part because Jobs worked outside of Apple, starting a new company from scratch. NEXT was all fringe and no center. It was the balance of center and fringe, of Scully and Jobs, that reinvented desktop computing around the world. That balance is where the magic lies.

In our personal relationships, the same dynamic holds true. We come to love people who are like us, but different, too, people who can offer security *and* spice, wisdom *and* wildness.

In family life, the same is true. How can a parent support a child? We tend to think that the more we focus on being good parents—thinking about and playing the "parent" role as intently as we can—the better we'll do. In the healthy family, the parents are the center; they're in charge of paying the bills, enforcing the rules, and husbanding the resources of the family, tremendously important tasks. It's the kids who are at the fringe, thinking new ideas, seeing the world in unexpected ways, and expressing dreams and desires that challenge even the most sensible plans. But for parents to have the most positive impact on their kids, they need to put aside the parent perspective now and then and think like children, to try to see the world from their kids' perspectives and tap into the youthful energies of young people fresh to the world. The idea isn't to abandon, or even to compromise, the traditional role of the parent. That's a role that must be played. The idea is to *add* a dimension of thought to the parent, to allow the parent to understand the child's goals—and to understand that children have dreams and desires that parents often can't anticipate or even imagine.

Understanding those dreams and desires is the key to understanding your children—and the key to being the best parent you can possibly be. A parent's gift to a child is the long process of helping the child become an adult. And a child's gift to a parent is helping the parent recapture a bit of the magic of seeing the world with new eyes. Both matter, and each gift needs the other in order to be complete.

THE DEAL THAT GOT AWAY: UNDERSTANDING THE STRONGER AND THE WEAKER

> *Why do so many deals go south? Why do so many people who share the same goals and* want *to agree wind up fighting instead? One key factor is that most people have trouble seeing the limits of their own strength, and wind up with unrealistic goals driven more by ego than by reality.*

Sometimes you can tell when everyone in the room wants to make a deal. After the bluster and the big claims, after the how-are-you's and the polite exchanges, the air in the room changes, the glimmer in everyone's eyes sharpens, and you know this won't be one of those pretend negotiations, all theater and in the end no deal. Instead, when everyone's serious, the collective will to deal sits in the room like an elephant. Everyone can smell it.

You might be negotiating the business deal of a lifetime—selling your company, or buying someone else's. Or making the case for a major bump in salary. Or maybe you're talking with your middle schooler about making a real effort to turn around those rotten grades and commit to schoolwork. Or it's the big negotiation to put limits on development in your town, or to recruit a new employer to the area.

If you've lived through any deals like these, you know that more often than not what seem to be real negotiations turn out just to be practice—on the other side of the table they're just here to learn, to get to know you, or to kill time. The buyer doesn't really want to buy—or doesn't have the money. It just feels good to go through the motions. Your kid isn't ready to get serious, he just wants you off his back. The town committee's got no intent of doing something new. They just want to hear you out, to give you your turn at the table before moving on to the next group.

So when deal time has really come, you can't just let it slip away. And yet more often than not the deals that could be done don't get done. Mom and Dad push their middle schooler too hard, and her defenses kick in and kill the deal. The seller adds trivial but deal-killing demands and the buyer walks away. Look closely at all the negotiations going on all around, and you'll see how large a portion of them go south.

Why? Why do people so often blow deals they really want? Why do they ask for too much, or ask for the right things in the wrong way? Tip O'Neill, one of the great American politicians of the twentieth century, has part of the answer. O'Neill earned a reputation as one of the classic deal makers and arm twisters of American public life. His greatest observation about deal-making is already a classic: "Politics," he quipped, "is the art of the possible." Plan your deal around asking for too much—or too little—and you show yourself to be out of touch with what's possible. Look hard at reality, understand the other guy's position, and you'll make the deals that would otherwise get away.

I can count dozens of major deals I've seen go south because someone at the table had no clue how the other guy saw himself. Almost every time, the deal blower was in a weak position and did not know it. He thought about the price he wanted not in terms of what the other party could pay, but in terms of how special he thought his own accomplishments had been. So instead of saying, "Well, you guys have only X cash on hand, so I'll take X now, and 2X more over time as this deal brings you new revenue," deal blowers say things like "You think I'm only worth X? You think ten years of my blood and sweat are only worth X? They're worth 3X or no deal."

The deal blower just does not understand what is possible, because he's stuck at the first level of thinking, always asking "How do I look? What am I worth?" He never sees the deal from the other side of the table, from the perspective of the person he's negotiating with. Getting to the second level of thinking doesn't help much either—at this level, negotiators run into a classic roadblock: they want to look strong to the rest of the world. They can't take stock of the true value of what they're selling, because they can never confess to being anything but strong. Yet knowing and being up-front about your weaknesses does not kill deals. If your view of your own weaknesses is a realistic one, you can turn that into a strength. And in every negotiation, one party is stronger than the other. Knowing where you stand, even if you're the weaker party, gives you real advantages. Pretending that you're something you're not is simply foolish, and leads you away from the path to success.

CASE STUDY: THE HUNDRED-BILLION-DOLLAR DEAL THAT GOT AWAY

> *IBM came knocking on the door of a little software company, wanting to do a deal but making some harsh demands at the same time. The software company's CEO was offended and walked away. So IBM went to the next little company on its list. There, Bill Gates was struggling to keep tiny Microsoft in business. So he took the terms IBM offered and parlayed that deal into a world-changing empire.*

One of the most stunning examples of the blown deal in our time is the contract that IBM wanted to sign with a small company called Digital Research, Inc., back in 1980. A couple of men in suits, emissaries of IBM's daring new business in Florida building personal computers, went out to see a man named Gary Killdall, the owner of Digital Research, to talk about IBM licensing Digital's disk operating system—basic software for making IBM's new desktop computers operate at the most basic level. Without the disk operating software, the computer could do nothing more than sit there on someone's desk. IBM was a classic big company, very sure of its power and not the kind of partner that expected to be gentle to small businesses it worked with. IBM had lots of money, though, and its negotiators suggested that the privilege and profits of working with IBM would be fair compensation for however much bullying the big company indulged in.

Killdall at Digital Research didn't see things that way. Like many software programmers, he acted as though he were the indispensable ingredient in his potential partner's plans. So when the men from IBM declared that they would not be able even to begin talking about the deal until Digital Research signed an onerous confidentiality and noncompete agreement, Digital walked away from the deal. Feeling strong, feeling satisfied with his own worth and status, Killdall took the stance that IBM needed him more than he needed IBM. When the billion-dollar corporation seemed not to agree, the deal was over before it began.

The next tiny company on whose door IBM knocked had a better sense of which party was the stronger and which was the weaker—at least, weaker for the moment. IBM tried out its nasty confidentiality agreement on a microscopic little business called Microsoft, and its founder, Bill Gates, signed it. He didn't actually have the software IBM wanted to buy, but said he did. Then he went out and bought the software from another little company. That let Gates deliver on his side of the deal with IBM that became the basis of Microsoft's global domination of the software business and Gates's personal $75 billion fortune.

In negotiating the deal, Gates actually took advantage of IBM's strength by letting the giant win the battle over price—he took under $100,000 for rights to MS-DOS—but he won the war over ultimate ownership of the software code. IBM saw little significance in Gates's desire to keep rights to sell the same software to other computer manufacturers. Big IBM planned to crush its competitors, so who cared if Gates had those rights? If IBM could squeeze a few more pennies out of Gates in the process by paying him even less for use of the code, why not? But IBM was wrong—and Microsoft went on to build a world-changing empire on IBM's mistake. Bill Gates's willingness to swallow his pride and accept the role of the weaker party was the beginning of it all.

The story of Microsoft illustrates how quickly the weaker party can become the stronger, once it stops pretending to be stronger than it is. To revisit Tip O'Neill's maxim, if politics is the art of the possible, once you make the best possible deal today, what's possible tomorrow expands almost infinitely. If you don't make the deal today, no new doors open. If you don't make the deal that's possible today, you don't get to play in the game that can lead to much bigger things tomorrow.

A Lesson from Plato: The Power of Purpose

> *Understanding where you're going is one of the best ways to make sure you get there. That's what purpose is all about: having an end in mind, and working a little bit longer, a little bit harder, to get there.*

When I worked as a business consultant, I saw the power of purpose all the time. People who could see the big picture had much greater ability to put up with the nonsense that pervades most large organizations—the rules and the meetings and the silly limitations that tend to grow inside big institutions. The people who couldn't cut it simply saw a series of disconnected actions that never made sense viewed in isolation. See the big picture, focus on the week and the month and year, and you can make it through the day. But if the day is all you've got, you wind up sacrificing long-term value for the sake of short-term satisfaction. And this applies at the top of the organizational chart just as much as it does at the bottom.

Take, for example, a fellow who led the New York area practice of a large international consulting firm, a decent enough fellow known among friends and enemies as the Rump. The Rump—short for RMP, or Regional Managing Partner—ran his regional office on several floors of a swanky high-rise. The handful of million-dollar-a-year partners in the firm enjoyed views of New York harbor and the hills of New Jersey. But most of the firm's office space was open, and the feeling was agricultural—acres and acres of cubicles in neat rows, waiting to be harvested. In those cubicles toiled the worker bees of the consulting world, tremendously well (if somewhat narrowly) educated people just on the border between youth and middle age, crunching numbers, writing reports, and trying with unbounded discipline to please their bosses.

The bosses lined the outer walls in their offices—small ones, actually—having graduated from their own cubes and found themselves neither fired nor recruited away from the firm but made, instead, into middle-rank partners. They did not strike visitors as happy people. Their offices were small because the man who ran New York for this firm—the Rump—wanted them to be out of the office as much as possible, visiting the clients they serve, billing for their time. "They want offices?" he asked. "They've got *great* offices, *beautiful* offices, all over town, out at the clients, but not for a minute more than they have to should they be in this office. Get them out. Get them billing. Don't let them get too comfortable."

The partners in New York worked for the Rump but each had his own book of business, his own claim on a number of clients, and could conceivably leave. The Rump had to keep these partners working hard, but he also had to keep them happy.

One bright day, I found myself sitting in the little glass-walled conference room next to the Rump's modest office, looking across the Hudson River at the giant neon "Colgate" sign on the Jersey waterfront waiting for the man to join us—me, his head of communications, and his chief of staff—to talk about a speech he was planning to give his partners. He wanted some help. He had a general sense of what he wanted to say, but he wanted to add something to the speech, to give it some weight, some kind of reference point beyond the obvious need to make more money and beat the wolfish competition.

He wanted, in short, to add some ideas.

He entered the room, a fireplug in a good suit, forceful but self-conscious, and asked no one in particular, "Where do we start?"

We started with his simple goals—to reinforce his authority among the senior consultants working for him, to build confidence, and to encourage a certain amount of change. The ground rules at the firm had changed in recent years. Things had gotten more competitive and intense, but also more profitable and just about everyone understood that clients were getting better service and more value. Still, some people in the organization were cynically expecting things to snap back to the old ways. They saw the new, higher standards in the office as a passing fad.

"Too many people here think it's a game," the Rump said. "They think that hard work is this year's big idea, that next year there'll be a new one." His chief of staff added, "Some of the people here welcome the change because they understand that there is a better way to run our business. Others see the pieces but not the whole. They don't think that the place we're trying to head is a real place."

That was it—the essential difference between the people who would live happily under the new regime and those who would not: it was a difference in understanding. The people who would thrive understood that there was a real ideal that the firm was striving for. They knew that the firm was working with a clear purpose these days. Those who did not get it were trapped within a vision of the future that had no ideal, no real purpose. To them, the future was just the present with a few changes laid on top. They did not understand that a coherent, better way to do business did in fact exist and was worth the struggle to make real.

Trying to explain these big ideas to his partners was a difficult task for the Rump. He needed a way to make clear the difference between real purpose and just aimless change. The best place to look, I suggested, was in the writings of Plato. And so, this quickly, sitting in the shiny offices of one of the world's largest consulting firms, we were in the world of Plato and his notion of the forms, or ideals.

Plato's notion of the forms is straightforward—for every object and idea that people can perceive or imagine, there is a pure and perfect version of that object or idea. So a tree growing from the ground is a variation on the form of the tree, the pure and perfect tree. As Socrates says in the *Republic*, talking with his friend Glaucon, when mathematicians puzzle out problems in geometry by drawing squares and circles and measuring their pieces, "they are thinking not of these, but of the ideals which they resemble; not of the figures which they draw, but of the absolute square and the absolute diameter."

So the executives working for the Rump who understood the vision and purpose of their boss—who understood that the whole process of change they had been living through was the product of their boss's vision—had an intuitive sense of Plato's forms. They were thinking not of the small changes unfolding close at hand, but of the ideals they represented—the ideals of efficiency and professional community that the Rump did in fact have in mind. They saw the difficult changes they faced today connected to a greater purpose that would become real tomorrow.

The executives who were unable to make that leap—who did not see the change unfolding around them as a process of getting closer to an ideal, but rather merely as a set of changes being made to a system they had become used to—were limited by their inability to think in Plato's terms, to see the ideal of a certain kind of organization that they could and should draw closer to.

Some partners thought the Rump's motives were crass—to squeeze more profitability from the organization, at the expense of the well-being (and the relative ease of life, day to day) of the old-timers at the firm. If they saw the specific effects of his actions as his principal motives, they could never trust him—he would never be exercising real leadership, but instead simply managing a series of alterations in work practice. But look at what Socrates has to say about the forms in his dialogue the *Phaedo*, talking with Cebes: "I stoutly contend that by beauty all beautiful things become beautiful." Socrates is talking about "beauty" as the form, the ideal of ordinary things that aspire toward the beautiful. In this dialogue, Socrates works out his notion that our visions of what is possible drive us to make those visions real. We are dreamers. We can imagine a better world, and because we can imagine it, we set out to make it so.

Another way to put this is to say that all things move from the weaker to the stronger, from the ordinary to the ideal. Why? Because humans are born with a sense of ambition, with a feeling that what we see around us is not as good as it could be, and therefore we wish to make it better.

As soon as the Rump could communicate these ideas, this sense of purpose, to his colleagues—the day he could lead them to believe that his changes and reforms were motivated by a clear belief that their firm could and should be better, not just more profitable but *better,* closer to an indelible image we all can imagine of the better state, the better firm—that would be his day of victory.

"I want this change," the Rump said, understanding Plato's lesson, "because it will make us a better firm. That's my message." His voice rose; he began to orate: "We have it within us to be a better firm, for each of us to be a better professional, and for all of us to make more money. That should be enough." He took a breath and turned to his chief of staff. "That's what I want the speech to say. 'Beauty is the cause of beauty' is maybe too much, but I like the theme that not one of us is as good as we can be yet, and that our changes are all about becoming what we all think we can be. Hit that private ambition, that little inkling that we can do more, that we are better than we seem to be. That's the point. That's the theme of the speech."

"It's about imagination," his communications director said. "I think that's the issue. Imagine what it is to be better. For the firm to be better, for the individual to be better. Fix in your mind what it looks like and feels like when all the pieces are in place, and we're at the perfect level. I think we need the speech to do that. Get the feeling, get the vision, of what exactly it will feel like when we get there. Get that ideal clearly enough said, or get the senior partners to look inside themselves and find their own images of themselves as heroes, and I think we can win them over."

Plato presents an almost religious vision of a world that our individual souls live in before we find human form in the ordinary world; in this world, we experience every object and every idea in its perfect form—love is love in its ideal state; the air is perfect, purest air; it is the notion of air and the essence of air without flaw. Among ordinary things, we live our physical lives in something like a fallen state, with vague yearnings and dissatisfactions that come, in fact, from our intuitive sense that things are not what they once were, that the ideals and objects of our lives are only imitations of better and more pure ideas and objects. And so we strive, with varying degrees of energy and success, to make what we have better, to come closer to the ideal states of things we once knew when we lived however briefly among the forms. The best among us, in Plato's view, feel that lack of perfection most strongly; the visionaries among us have the clearest sense that better is possible, and the clearest sense of how to push or pull our world closer to the world of the forms. The people who become angry at mediocrity, the people who know that what they hold in their hands is not what it could be and cannot restrain themselves from trying to make it better, are Plato's hope for the future of a more meaningful, more satisfying, and more virtuous life.

Talking about these ideas for an hour or so left all of us in that conference room the challenging task of putting these ideas into a speech, and making them relevant to management consulting partners. But I think we all felt that the partners would get it—Plato's belief that people are born with the ambition to make things better, and live better lives because of that ambition, would resonate with these hard-driving overachievers who, after all, spent most of their days telling the leaders of large businesses how to do things better.

And so the speech the Rump gave mentioned Plato, only a bit but to strong effect, and at least a couple of his colleagues seemed swayed. They understood, I think, that he was not moving away from the firm's past as much as he was moving toward its future. They saw that he had a purpose. The Rump convinced his partners that aspiration toward an ideal was a noble thing, a thing worth getting up in the morning and coming to work for.

I left that meeting remembering a day years earlier, walking through an empty and long boarded-up old store on a quiet street in a far corner of New York. The man I was with, a relative, stepped over the years of garbage strewn beside overturned tables and boxes of old tableware, empty bottles that had filled with mold from years of the musty atmosphere in what turned out to be a failed lunch restaurant, now long shuttered.

My relative's eyes gleamed. He could see the place, restored as an old-fashioned sweet shop—the kind of place he had stopped in after school in the 1940s for an egg cream and a candy. He could hear Glenn Miller's big band playing as it had played back then; he could smell the sugary smells of the old sweet shops in his boyhood neighborhood and see the characters of his early life filling the store he would re-create.

Every change he would make as he restored that little storefront would be far more significant than someone seeing him work could know. Only someone who understood his thoughts, his interior vision of what the corner sweet shop had once been, could know that the changes were all small pieces that added up to a whole that was already fully conceived in his mind.

It was that whole, that vision of the sweet shop he would bring from the memory of his childhood into physical existence on a street in New York, that drove him. That was his vision. That was his purpose. It was the reason he worked so hard, and the reason his work was so satisfying. "By beauty," said Socrates, "all beautiful things become beautiful." The invisible ideal, the vision, of what a thing can be, helps to make it so. And because of my relative's vision of what he was building, he built. The image of what he would make real was the very cause of his work, and it would eventually be, in a happy end for him, its own reward and fulfillment.

THE LEAP OF FAITH: CONNECTING INSIGHT TO RELATIONSHIPS

> *Even after you do everything right, powered by ambition and filled with insight, you'll find limits to your success. At times, you'll need to take a leap of faith to get to the next level.*

Without a doubt, one of Bill Gates's secret weapons as he built Microsoft was sheer brain power. He's one smart guy. Most of the rest of us don't come close to the intellect that Gates and his top lieutenants possess, but we use the intellect we've got to propel our work and build our own successes. In fact, as a general rule, most people view their success at work as a function of brains. And it's true that day in and day out, we rely on reason—careful thought, observation, the weighing of evidence—to make the decisions that keep our lives moving ahead. But most of us also have some degree of faith in our lives. We make some decisions not based on reason but based on feelings of the heart and of the spirit—feelings like love, loyalty, and inspiration. That fact is crucial, because reason has its limits, something even Bill Gates would admit.

The greatest insights about what faith can do that reason cannot came in the early nineteenth century, courtesy of the philosopher Søren Kierkegaard. But before you encounter Kierkegaard's ideas, you have to encounter the man, a hunchback philosopher given to long solitary walks in all weather through his chilly hometown of Copenhagen, Denmark. In one of his books, Kierkegaard describes himself sitting in a park in Copenhagen smoking a cigar, looking around and seeing great works of engineering—new towers, new bridges—rising up around him, the work of men of his own generation, men he had known in university. The time was coming, he wrote, for him to make his own great contribution to Copenhagen. But unlike the contributions of his peers, his would not make life easier for the citizens of his community, but more difficult.

What did he mean by that? That he would not try to help people solve their short-term problems—problems like, how can I get from here to there?—but that he would help them rethink (or think about for the first time) the very ideas they base their lives on. And while everyone can recognize the value of short-term gains that new bridges and the like provide, an awful lot of people see the kinds of fundamental changes that Kierkegaard was interested in—changes like abandoning illusions and seeing yourself in an objective light—as painful. We don't want to give up our illusions, and often we don't want to admit that we're capable of accomplishing more than we're accomplishing at the moment. It's just hard, hard to shake off the false personal limits we become used to over time.

Kierkegaard's writings were focused on shaking off those limits, and he was right that many readers thought he was a troublemaker, just making their lives harder.

But more than trouble, Kierkegaard brought his readers real wisdom. He is the writer who coined the term "the leap of faith," and that notion is precisely where insight and relationships connect. Kierkegaard was writing in an era that valued reason. It was the force behind the technological revolution of his time— all that bridge and tower building. Many religious thinkers of the era declared that reason itself could lead to religious feeling and perhaps even to salvation. But Kierkegaard knew better, and in his books he described the limits of reason and the great spiritual rewards that could come only after a man or woman had the courage to take reason as far as it would go, and then leap into the uncertainty of faith. For Kierkegaard, faith is what begins where reason ends.

Now, Kierkegaard was clear about his faith—he meant faith in God, a religious commitment. But Kierkegaard was a rebel, and he made church authorities nervous. Truly original thinkers often have that effect. Kierkegaard was saying that faith is hard, not easy. That its rewards are uncertain and its cost might be terribly high. And this might well be so when we speak of faith in God.

But without a doubt, faith in other people is a simpler matter: its rewards are certain. Faith in other people is what helps you reach your practical, earthly goals when cold hard reason has run out of gas. Faith in other people completes the circle of sharing our gains and dedicating our ambitions to helping others. It is, in fact, both the starting point and the finish line for reaching our goals.

Martin Luther King, describing the logic of his nonviolent protest movement, often said "the ends are pre-existent in the means." He meant that you have to make your methods reflect what you are trying to achieve in the long run. If you are after peace, your methods must be peaceful. If you are after justice, your methods must be just. And if you are after helping others, your methods must be helpful—you have to align what you do with what you believe. You have to climb the ladder of success with your hand out to help others all the way up. Why? For two reasons. First, it's the right thing to do—it makes your faith in other people visible and real. Second, it works. Helping others makes you stronger. It helps you win.

THREE LESSONS FROM SØREN KIERKEGAARD

Reason and insight will only take you so far.

When reason ends, faith can begin.

Real faith in other people is a risk and takes courage, but it unlocks immense new possibilities.

The Power of Purpose

THE GREATEST PRAYER

*Thomas Merton, a twentieth-century Christian philoso-
pher, offered a powerful lesson in paying attention to the
spark of purpose and power that we sometimes feel ignite
within us.*

Thomas Merton was a Christian monk, a scholar of literature,
an essayist, and a poet. He was an important voice in American
literature and culture in the 1950s and 1960s, and, for a monk
who had taken a vow of silence, he had a lot to say and got special dispensation to say it often. He wrote about war and peace,
about religion and secular society, and about literature. Every
now and then, when things in my life are going so well that I
feel like I have to thank someone, or something, for the great
things I've been given, I think about this simple statement Merton once made: "The greatest prayer is the impulse to pray."

That means a great deal to me, because I have felt it so often,
that impulse to pray. Not the impulse to join an order, or even
to pick up a book and read a prayer. Just an impulse to say thank
you, to recognize that I am one small part of a larger story, and
lucky to be here. Many would say that this feeling should lead
me to join in a more formal kind of worship, to connect with a
church or religious movement, to seek and heed the teaching of
a religious leader. And that may well be the best advice out
there. But Merton's modest statement captures something that
I cling to—something that has a lot to do with living with a
purpose. Merton's teaching makes the point that something
very personal, and very real, is at the root of the most powerful
spiritual feelings. Something spontaneous—something you
feel even though no one else witnesses you feeling it, even

though you win no points and get no external reward. There's just that little spark, that little impulse to reach out to something bigger and feel that connection.

And living life with a purpose works in much the same way. Movements and monuments, orders and orthodoxies may well guide you to a fine purpose and help you discover that you are indeed connected to every soul around you. But the greatest prayer is the impulse to pray, and the greatest purpose is the purpose that begins inside you and rises up to meet the world. It can't come to you because someone else points to you and tells you you have a purpose. It can't come to you from your parents, your spouse, or your children. It comes *to* you *from* you. It is a gift you give to yourself, a choice you make with your mind and your soul that stirs you to listen with great care to others, and to reach out. When you feel that impulse, when you hear yourself saying "I can help others," you know you're feeling that greatest feeling, and finding that greatest purpose.

CRITICAL INSIGHTS: THE BIG FIVE

Three levels of thinking.

Focus on the war, not on the battle.

Be at the center AND at the fringe.

Know who is the stronger and who is the weaker in every negotiation (the art of the possible).

Where reason ends, faith can get you the rest of the way.

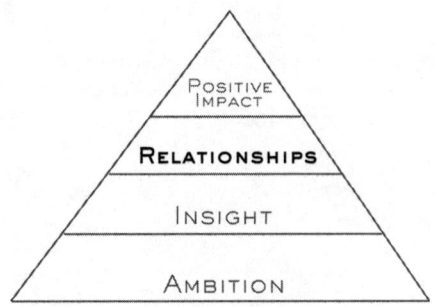

PART IV

RELATIONSHIPS: WITHOUT RELATIONSHIPS WITH OTHERS, NOTHING ELSE IS POSSIBLE

Relationships can make all the difference between reaching your goals and merely coming close. We all know people who seem to have every tool they need to succeed—but having all the skills and insights in the world means nothing if you can't connect, if you don't know how to be part of a team, and if all your successes are lonely ones that you don't get to share with others.

Mastering relationships is the third level of the pyramid, building on the power of ambition and the skills of insight to connect with others.

* * *

Some people just can't help but push other people away. They do it by falling so in love with themselves that they have no compassion left for others. They do it by keeping secrets, by hoarding the rewards they earn when they win, and by failing to learn from their mistakes when they lose. They alienate others because they have not learned to be humble, and because they cannot see the spark of precious humanity in every man and woman they meet.

Others people are lonely for other reasons—they see the value of others, they want to connect, but they just don't know how. Without close role models from early in life, it's difficult to learn how to listen to others with skill and compassion, to find the delicate balance between giving and taking that makes relationships work.

The truth is, the skills of relating to others are the most crucial skills to success, period. Without them nothing else is possible. Without them you will not win, and without them you will do no good for others. The crucial skills are about sharing every gain, rejecting every urge to keep secrets, always building teams, learning to listen, and balancing giving and taking—hard things for most people to do. But when you see how much these skills do to help you win the essential victories, they become much easier to master.

8

THE THREE CRITICAL
RELATIONSHIP SKILLS

PUTTING YOUR INSIGHTS TO WORK—USING THEM TO reach your goals and to help others—begins with a leap of faith, with a conviction that other people are important and deserve great respect and attention. No one can prove this; it's not a position that comes from the application of reason. It's a matter of faith, faith in people.

Three practical principles about dealing with people express this faith and are powerful tools for reaching your goals. The first is Share Every Gain. The second is No Secrets. And the third is Always Build Teams.

THE THREE CRITICAL RELATIONSHIP SKILLS

Share Every Gain.

No Secrets.

Always Build Teams.

SHARE EVERY GAIN

Whatever victories you win will always be incomplete until you share them with people you care about.

Share Every Gain is a principle that does not need a lot of explaining. You've probably felt the impulse behind it—the impulse to pick up the phone and call someone, maybe your spouse, maybe one of your parents, maybe a good friend—when something wonderful and unexpected happens. The success you feel is incomplete until you share the news with people you care about. That gut feeling is positive, but it sits at the first and second levels of thinking, at the level of the question "How do I feel about myself?" and at the level of the question "How do others feel about me?"

I pick up the phone to call my wife or my father when I get a big promotion in part because the promotion is an affirmation of my worth. My message is, "Hey, look at me! I'm a vice president!" I need an audience for that. I also want people I care about to know that I'm viewed with respect by my bosses and colleagues, and maybe to respect me a bit more themselves. But these desires don't do me or anyone else much good in the long run. It's only when I take that good news and find a way to make it pay off for others that it really makes me stronger and helps others reach their own goals. That might mean something as simple as telling my friend when I call him with news about my promotion, "I want to let you know what your help and support have done for me—I got the big job." Or it might mean that with my new job I'm going to use the practical gains coming my way to do something of value for someone who needs my help.

Here's an example: I have a friend who is the head of the technology division of a multibillion-dollar entertainment business. As I was getting to know him, he told me about his family. His sister, he said, is married to a schoolteacher and is one of the happiest people he knows. He told me where she lives, and I mentioned that it sounded like a place where a schoolteacher couldn't likely afford a comfortable house—it was too expensive. Well, he mentioned, he'd bought them a house.

I love that story, and it always makes me want to run out and buy *my* sister a house (it would be doubly expensive for me: I've got two sisters). I keep coming to the same conclusion when I think about my friend buying his sister a house—*that* is what money is for; *that* is what success is about. And that's an example of elevating the urge to share news of your victories up to the third level of thinking—the level at which you are always asking, How do others see themselves? What do they think of as *their* biggest needs and goals?

Of course, you don't have to spend money to do this. Sharing your time, sharing your ideas, and sharing your passion can be just as important. Just got a nice block of time off from work? Showing up for your sister's birthday though she lives five hundred miles away can be just as valuable as spending money on her—perhaps even more valuable. Practicing your listening skills? Listening to your sister's dreams and plans—maybe at greater length than you'd be inclined to if you were thinking only of yourself—is also a great way to share your strength.

People who tithe to their churches exhibit this ethic of sharing every gain; they share their success with the church and the people who are helped by it. In the Jewish tradition, the Hebrew bible tells landowners to keep a small part of their fields unharvested after every growing season, so that the poor can come and harvest a bit for themselves, allowing the poor shared gain, and allowing them the dignity of working a bit for their food. Islam, too, places a tremendous emphasis on hospitality—sharing your home, your food, and protection from the harsh forces of the world is one of the most sacred obligations for Muslim believers. Using your strength to serve others is at the heart of that religion's traditions.

Many towns across the United States have what they call "Carnegie libraries." Andrew Carnegie, the industrialist of the late nineteenth and early twentieth centuries made this deal to share his wealth: any community that would agree to pay the running costs of a library would get, for free from Carnegie's personal fortune, a new building to house it. That was one of his visions for sharing his gains. Bill Gates, founder of Microsoft, used his wealth to update those libraries by paying for Internet connectivity to any public library that was not already wired in the late 1990s.

Walk by any school in a poor neighborhood after classes end, and you're likely to see volunteers in after-school centers, helping children with their homework. Those people are sharing their good fortune, even if they can't write big checks like Carnegie and Gates. Go to any park on a sunny day, and look around at the adults taking time out of their lives to play with young children. Some are parents, some are nannies, but some are uncles and cousins and neighbors, giving moms and dads a break and sharing their strength.

Sharing every gain is an ethic that gives you specific challenges. Having a new baby is a wonderful thing—how will you share that gain? Acquiring a new skill—playing the guitar, or speaking French—is a gain. How will you share it? Winning a new account is a gain that you need to share. So is getting a big new office at work, and being invited to address your firm's board of directors. How can you share these gains? Even winning an argument is a gain (and losing an argument can be a bigger gain, if you learn something important in the process). How will you share that? The answers are infinitely varied. It's the question that always stays the same and always remains essential.

GIVING AND TAKING

Helping others is a powerful experience, but at times the best help we can give others is to let them help us.

A very accomplished friend of mine recently told me about a difficult colleague he'd had at a financial consulting firm. "He was a monster, always taking credit for other people's ideas, never recognizing the good things other people were doing all around him, generally making the place miserable. Worst of all, he really didn't seem to think anyone else in the company had anything to offer him. He didn't want to learn from anyone, didn't want to share, didn't want to work in teams." My friend was working up a head of steam, painting a picture of this unsavory character. But he paused for a moment in the telling of the tale to add an important detail. "Except . . . except for one fellow. One guy in the office broke through and actually had a good relationship with this rotten egg. I remember, in fact, pulling him aside and asking him how he'd done it, how he'd proven himself worthy of a bit of this hotshot's time and attention. 'What in the world did it take to show that you were hot stuff enough to get him to take some notice? What did you have to show him from your bag of tricks?' And he said something beautiful then, he said, 'It was exactly the opposite. I didn't show him anything. I asked him, a couple of times, to show me something. I didn't try to work with him, just to be his audience. I asked him for a little help with a project I knew he'd have totally wired. I let him showboat. And it was beautiful. Not only did he really have some good things to say, he was, for a fleeting second, really happy. That was worth seeing.'"

Years ago, I saw a similar drama unfold on the observation deck of the Empire State Building in New York. The Empire State Building draws tourists from all over the world, and one particular family was amusing themselves during the long wait for the express elevator to the observation deck by trying to teach a little girl—she must have been four or five—how to count in English. I still have no idea where they were from—their accents were vaguely Eastern European, but the language they spoke with one another was impenetrable to me.

The young girl's mother held her hand, and another man and woman, seeming to be their hosts, perhaps fellow countrymen who'd settled in New York, were keeping everyone laughing by counting from one to ten in English and trying to get the little girl past three. "One, tao, tree . . ." She enjoyed the crazy sounds of this new language that filled the air all around her. At least for a while. Soon enough, though, she began to understand that even though she was the star of this little drama, what was really amusing was that she was getting things wrong. Her happiness began to fade, and her struggle to keep from crying was becoming clear to everyone around her.

But then one of her hosts had a brainstorm. It turned out that he was not a native of the girl's home country and had just as hard a time with their language as the girl was having with English. Just as she teetered on the brink of tears, he stuck out his fist and started counting in her mysterious language. One finger popped out, and he said, bright and clear, something that sounded to me like "Egg!" The girl stopped whining and looked up at his finger, and his face. Then he stuck out another finger and said, "Po!" With that she got it—he was trying to count. But pathetically. She smiled as he stuck out a third finger: "Harum!" She laughed. Her mother laughed. This guy was a mess.

Then the girl pulled down his hand and helped him start over, teaching him to count with her untroubled voice, the voice of a girl who knew what she was doing and might, as an act of generosity, help this foolish man who could not—how was this even possible?—count to ten in the most natural language in the world.

That was a lovely moment. The man understood that this little girl was exhausted by others trying to teach her, and that the greatest gift he could offer her in this crazy new country of Empire State Buildings and yellow taxis and crowded skies was his own need to be helped along, bit by bit, to count to ten. He let her help him, and that made all the difference on that sunny, windy day.

No Secrets

> *Secrets make you feel stronger, but they undermine trust*
> *and keep you locked into thinking at the lowest levels.*

No Secrets is a pretty simple principle, though it's one of the hardest to follow. People all around you will ask you to keep secrets, and it's difficult to do the right thing without seeming to reject their values. But secrets do harm, without a doubt. You can imagine the harm they do within families, and if you've worked in an organization of any size, you've probably seen the harm they do at work, too.

Secrets are all about the first and second levels of thinking. In fact, keeping secrets prevents people from reaching the third level of thinking.

At the first level, it's easy to feel that the secret makes you stronger in your own eyes. At the second level, whoever knows—or even suspects—that you know secrets will see you a little differently. They'll trust you less but fear you more. How much closer does that get you to your goals? Not one bit.

When someone tells you a secret, ask yourself what that secret means to the teller—how that person looks to him- or herself. Only then can you start turning the bad news—secrets are always bad news—into something better. Let the secret teller know that you don't do secrets, but that you can help with the underlying problem the secret represents.

Those underlying problems can be very important. When you hear a secret, or reach the conclusion that someone you care about or work with is a secret keeper, try to answer the question of why that person likes secrets. One clue to answering that question is that different kinds of secrets represent different kinds of problems.

A common kind of secret is embarrassing information about others. Someone tells you, "Did you hear about Dave? It's disgusting! But don't tell anyone else." These secrets are generally a form of aggression, revealing anger at the person the secret is about. How can you help? Figure out why that anger is there, and try to make a positive difference in whatever conflict is causing the anger. Your greatest contribution might be to listen to the secret keeper and help him feel that he's taken seriously. But Dave's private life is, ultimately, not your concern. Helping your colleague with his feelings of anger is the better contribution for you to make.

Another common kind of secret involves embarrassing information about the secret teller him- or herself. In this case, the immediate question that should come to mind is twofold: Why are you doing something you aren't proud of, and why are you telling me about it? In many cases, the secret here is a classic cry for help, and you might find that as a friend you can indeed help by talking and affirming the secret teller's instinct that the behavior is wrong. In other cases, the secret teller might be fishing for someone with similarly bad judgment, and you need to be clear about where you draw your boundaries.

But in all of these cases, the best path lies in rejecting the urge to keep secrets. That policy not only keeps you out of trouble, but it also gains you an opportunity to make a positive difference by helping the secret tellers take a step away from their urges to keep secrets, too.

Of course, No Secrets does not mean that you need to be compulsively forthcoming with news about everything you do and know, but it does mean that you need to be honest about what information you can and can't share, and that everyone in your family, at work, and in your community understands how and why you share information. That's part of defining the difference between keeping a secret and keeping a confidence.

My teenage daughter, for example, confides in her aunt. But the ground rules are clear—any information that my sister learns that suggests that my daughter might be at any risk of harm is not going to be kept secret. And there have been times my daughter has told my sister things that she must have known my sister would share with me and my wife. I suspect my daughter wanted us to know these things so that we could help her, though it felt impossible for her to tell us directly.

Another example: at the graduate school I led, we worked for a long time to share more budget information with department heads than we'd shared in the past. The department heads would have liked to see all of the graduate school budgets, line by line. But we had a clear expectation of confidentially regarding salaries. So we created a modified open budget—some lines weren't there, to respect people's privacy about salaries, but we shared a lot more financial information than we'd ever shared in the past, and the department heads felt more empowered in the budgeting process. They understood more about how we spent money, and about the ways their departments fit into the larger picture of the school. This wasn't easy to pull off. Some people pushed hard for us to disclose more and more financial information. But so long as we were acting in good faith, trying to disclose more rather than less, we put ourselves on the right side of the line between secrets and confidences.

In my experience, more people are on the other side of that line, at least once in a while, than most ethical leaders would like. The urge to keep secrets is natural—you want to hide your mistakes, avoid losing whatever it is your secrets might jeopardize, and enjoy the jolt of emotional power that comes from knowing something others don't. And in organizations and families that aren't well balanced—where individuals are unfairly punished for their faults and failings; where ridicule is accepted; where trust is low—secrets can provide great short-term gain. But in the long run they create distance between people and inevitably result in more harm than good. In part this is because secrets by their nature leak. Someone tells me a secret they learned from someone else and swears me to silence. But I tell one person—someone I'd trust with my life—and swear him to silence. Then he tells the person he'd trust with his life, and soon everyone and their uncles know the secret.

SECRETS THAT BREAK APART TEAMS

> *Why do people break apart teams with secrets? Sometimes for what they see as personal gain (though that gain is usually an illusion), sometimes to express anger (even if that anger is really about something unconnected to the team), and sometimes because a team is broken and needs to be shaken up.*

One of the worst effects of secrets is that they often break apart teams—work teams, families, couples, and others. Many of us have seen what happens when trust vanishes in a family, a relationship, or a workplace. It's not pretty.

So why do people try to fracture teams with secrets? Sometimes for personal gain—they might be out of favor in the team and feel that change could make things better. Or there might be issues of aggression driving the secrets. And in some cases, of course, the team might simply be doing the wrong thing, and the people in it could be better off in a new group.

In almost all of these cases you have the opportunity to help build a *better* team. You might find that by being open with others about what's going on, you can help slow or stop the fracturing of the team (disrupters of teams are often driven by emotion, and lack long-term commitment to causing trouble; a little affirmation of their goals goes a long way). Or you might find that there is a legitimate role for creating new teams, and that by talking about this openly you can find a team to join that suits you better than the one you're on.

Far better than shaking up troubled teams by keeping secrets, though, is understanding how and why teams work. Work at fixing the broken teams, and building new teams on sound principles, and you'll be taking giant steps toward *all* of your long-term goals.

Finding New Glue for New Teams: If You Can't Sell Together, Sail Together

> *When you can't get your team to work together on your main task, look for other opportunities to share risk and build trust. Get away from your expected roles, and get people relating to one another with the casual support that comes naturally, but which is often strained in tight social groups and the workplace.*

Here's a nice shorthand for a good strategy to fix a broken team: maybe we can't sell together, but we can sail together. Say you have someone disrupting a sales team at work. If you can find a common enterprise that has nothing to do with selling—and sailing is a great choice—you can share risk and build trust that way, and develop habits of teamwork likely to carry over back in the office and the field.

Sailing is a great parallel activity because it does, in fact, involve real risk. This also explains the popularity of the adventure-course model of leadership training—tie people together (often literally), put them in danger, and they'll be forced to rely on one another. Now, sometimes these adventure courses backfire, because they *reveal* lack of trust without *healing* it.

That raises the vital question, why are so many people unwilling to exercise trust in relationships at work? The answer is usually straightforward: they have no faith that if they share your risks they'll share your gain. And that's the vital connection between Share Every Gain and No Secrets—if you start off sharing every gain, over time even many of the hard cases will begin to trust you, and their secrets will fade, because they know that when they share risk with you, they'll share in the payoff, too.

Are some people incapable of this kind of growth over time? Yes indeed. Can you tell the difference between that minority and the majority who will respond positively over time? Only if you make the commitments to doing relationships the right way, by sharing every gain and keeping no secrets.

The same holds true among friends, at work, and even in the most intimate relationships. In fact, new research into why marriages break up has suggested a fascinating insight: in marriages that survive, spouses fight just as often, and about the same things, as spouses in marriages that *don't* last. The differences between lasting marriages and couples heading for divorce aren't in the negatives; there isn't *less* fighting in the lasting marriages. The differences are in the positives—there is *more* laughing, more casual physical contact, more shared enthusiasm in the marriages that last. So when there's stress in a relationship about money, to take a common enough example, the hope for that marriage probably does not lie in directly changing how the spouses talk about money, but in how they talk about other things—not the selling, but the sailing, or in this case, not the earning and spending, but the long walks and quiet talks.

The trick to making a typical marriage work, it seems, is the balance of the good against the bad, the sharing of the whole package. If you can't help but fight over money, but then don't balance that out by sharing the small joys of a life truly shared, you might think that money problems have sunk your marriage, when in fact it's the lack of the good, not the presence of the bad, that makes all the difference. It's the total package that leads to success, the sharing of whole lives. If you give your spouse only part of yourself, if you keep secrets, if you try too hard to put only certain pieces of your personal puzzle into your marriage, you'll make a happy ending harder to find.

So the best prescription for a marriage struggling because of conflict over issue X isn't necessarily to hit that issue head-on, but to focus, too, on issues Y and Z, things that both partners agree on that help build the habits of caring and mutual support.

American poet Walt Whitman understood better than anyone how complicated these kinds of personal relationships can be, and he wrote about these complications more than one hundred years ago in his long poem "Song of Myself."

The Three Critical Relationship Skills

Do I contradict myself?
Very well then I contradict myself,
(I am large, I contain multitudes.)

In a sense, we all contain multitudes, and we all contradict ourselves. It's a good thing, too. If you hit a roadblock relating to someone you care about, don't fall under the illusion that this person is 100 percent disagreeable. Whitman's advice is right on point: this problem person contains multitudes, too. Explore those multitudes that are hidden inside, and you'll probably find some positive qualities and enough common ground to build the beginnings of a positive relationship. That relationship might not relate to what you think of as your main connection with this person, be it shared work or living together as roommates or even marriage, but there's probably something positive there that you can find. If you can't sell together, try sailing together. If you can't find common ground sharing a refrigerator, try sharing a meal at a restaurant, or a baseball game. You've got multitudes of ways to build that connection.

THE POWER OF POETRY

With precious few words, the right poem at the right
moment can speak with the clearest of voices and help us
see new things in the world and in the people we care
about.

I actually think about poetry a lot and find the wisdom of poets useful in my personal relationships and in my work life. One of the most popular American poems—a simple sketch by poet William Carlos Williams—brilliantly captures the struggles of sharing a life with someone you care about. It's titled "This Is Just to Say" and reads, in its entirety,

> *I have eaten*
> *the plums*
> *that were in*
> *the icebox*
>
> *and which*
> *you were probably*
> *saving*
> *for breakfast*
>
> *Forgive me*
> *they were delicious*
> *so sweet*
> *and so cold*

For me, this is a love poem. I picture the poem as a note—a scrap of paper in the fruit bin in the refrigerator. I can imagine someone buying two fat, juicy plums on the way home from work on a hot, hot day, thinking that they'll taste so wonderfully good, but then thinking that, in fact, after spending the night in the icebox, they'd be so much better. All night, dreams of cold, sweet plums swirl about the house. The next morning this innocent plum buyer walks into the kitchen, grabs the handle on the door to the icebox, opens the icebox, opens the fruit bin, and finds—horrors!—not plums, but a note: "This is just to say, I have eaten the plums . . ."

Why is this a love poem? For two reasons: first, because sharing a life with someone means, inevitably, sacrificing sweet things now and then for the sake of the larger relationship. It might be a bit of privacy that is lost, or a picture you love that will never find its way to hanging on the wall because your partner hates it, or those tasty sweets that you left in the kitchen but forgot to put a big sign on saying DON'T EAT THIS. So the frustration of the person who is left without plums is familiar, and a fine symbol of the sacrifices that come with shared lives. No one is perfect, we intrude in the lives of people we love, and we need to be forgiven now and then. Forgiveness, it turns out, is one of the highest forms of love.

Even more powerful, though, is the quick feeling I get every time I read this poem: well, I hope you enjoyed them. This is the same feeling a parent gets taking off his jacket on a cold, cold day, and wrapping it around his child. It is the same feeling a spouse gets when she takes that last bit of ice cream and spoons it into her partner's mouth—too bad I can't enjoy this, but your pleasure means something to me, too. This poem captures that feeling for me, that moment when one partner thinks, first, how rotten that I can't eat my plums, but then has a bit of shared joy, tasting what the other partner has tasted through some magic of love.

There's more to poetry than love, though. In fact, I've found that when it comes to business and money, the right poem can offer more practical help—and more sustaining energy—than your average master's degree in business administration.

Take the case of a young man I've known for a few years. Call him Bob. Bob was a student of mine at Columbia University in New York during a semester in which I told my students that anyone who would accompany me on foot from Columbia, near the top of Manhattan island, down to the Brooklyn Bridge, about nine miles south, and recite from memory twenty lines of Whitman's poetry would be the beneficiary of major extra credit points. Bob was one of the handful who came along and proclaimed their lines of verse on the bridge—including those lines about containing multitudes. Years later, I was raising money for a business from venture capitalists and got a call from my investment banker. Someone at one of New York City's hot VC outfits wanted to take a meeting and consider investing. That someone turned out to be Bob. After a number of interesting jobs in other fields, he'd landed a plum spot as a junior venture capitalist. And he had Walt Whitman to thank, proving the practical value of poetry. Bob was interviewing with the founding honcho of the VC firm and he got the logical question. "You're obviously very bright and accomplished, but you've bounced from field to field, from international trade to consulting to city government. How do I know you really want to be a venture capitalist?" He responded by quoting Whitman, those very lines from the Brooklyn Bridge: "Do I contradict myself? Well then, I contradict myself. I contain multitudes." The big VC was a literary sort himself, and he gave Bob the job. (Bob, in turn, decided not to give me the money I was after, but that's another story.)

FROM "ALWAYS BE CLOSING" TO ALWAYS BUILD TEAMS

Teams are the ticket to long-term success—teams of people invested in one another's success expand your reach, enlarge your wisdom, and help you keep your bal-

ance in hard times. Teams are all about the balance be-
tween service and success—the more you give when
you're part of a team, the more you get.

"First prize, the Cadillac. Second prize, steak knives. Third prize, you're fired." Actor Alec Baldwin spoke these words with a murderous smirk in the classic American sales movie *Glengarry Glen Ross*, about a group of small-time real-estate hustlers. That line captured the spirit of many sales organizations, the "what have you done for me lately" mind-set that helps keep numbers high in the short run but tends to crush all but the most competitive salespeople and creates a brutal work environment. Another line Baldwin, playing a sales consultant, drove home was "A, B, C—Always Be Closing." I've heard lots of salespeople use that phrase with a straight face, and in some situations I imagine it suits them well, but I know that in many others it can be poison. Always Be Closing means always think about the money. It means think short term. And the best salespeople know that the real money is in the long term.

So I'd vote to replace Always Be Closing in the sales vocabulary—and the vocabulary of every family and every community—with Always Build Teams. Closing is about success today. Teams are about success tomorrow. And the practice of *always* building teams is about success forever.

Most of us had our first exposure to teams in the school yard—we fell into teams for ball games and, at times, just to note the difference between kids we liked and kids we didn't. Organized sports drive home the idea that you're on only one team at a time, and that the purpose of Team A is to beat Team B. But teams work in other ways, too. Teams share strength and wisdom. They help people win bigger victories and share their gains. And they give us the close human contact and shared purpose that we all need to live full lives.

The most memorable bit of team building I ever witnessed took place when I was very young, no more than four years old. It was a snowy winter, and a heavy storm had just dumped almost two feet of snow on my neighborhood in Brooklyn. We lived in a little house on a street that was short one driveway—between our house and our neighbor's was a skinny strip of pavement, the width of a single car, leading to two garages in a shared backyard. Two houses, two garages, but only one driveway between us. Our neighbor, an elderly physician named Dr. Schneider, solved the problem by parking his tiny Volkswagen on his front lawn. But that winter day, a solid wall of snow and ice hemmed his car in and seemed to dictate an afternoon of soup and hot chocolate at home. But then Dr. Schneider got a call—a patient needed him. My father was outside shoveling along with a few neighbors digging out their own houses. Word spread among the adults that the doctor needed to get his car out, but the snow in front of his house would take an hour to clear. One of the men did some quick math—maybe seven strong-enough fellows out there, and one car that weighed, what, a thousand pounds? "Let's pick it up," he suggested, and after a collective chuckle, they circled the little car, everyone took a handful of bumper or car door, and as I stood on my front lawn I witnessed what looked like a miracle—the men of Coleridge Street picked up Dr. Schneider's car and carried it into the middle of the road. The doctor hopped in with his little black bag and sped away to heal the sick.

The men stood around very pleased with themselves, huffing steam clouds into the air, feeling the kind of proud connection among neighbors that we too seldom feel. This team of men came together and did something brave and important, bound to help others. How did they do it? First, they knew and trusted one another. Second, they had a high purpose—not one of them doubted the importance of getting the doctor on the road to do his work. Trust and high purpose were essential to the task.

But they weren't enough. Would any one of the men have thought of trying to lift the car by himself? Certainly not. The elegant—even heroic—solution to this problem was entirely a matter of teamwork. The team was more than a tool for solving a problem; it was also the source of the vision for the solution. The fact of a team standing at the ready was what led to the thought that, hey, we can just lift that darned car and get the doctor on the road. The value of teams, then, lies not only in what they can do, but how they elevate our thinking. If we make thinking in terms of teams more of a natural habit, our ambitions will rise, we'll do more good, and we'll have more meaningful moments like that great day in the snow when I was a small boy.

How, exactly, can you build teams? At every important juncture, look for people who can help you reach your goals, and people you can help in return. Work hard at helping other people succeed. And work hard at getting other people to invest in *your* success—invest in their ideas, their energy, their contacts, and their resources. Open yourself up to as much help from others as you can, even when you think you can manage just fine on your own.

At work, the process of building teams should begin even before your first day at any job. Opening new doors to landing a new job in the first place is a team effort, if you're smart.

THE WORK TEAM

Understanding the culture of the workplace is a team effort, too, and for sure building your success over the long term is a team effort as well. Here's how these three kinds of team building might work.

Opening the Doors

Whether you're looking for a job, angling for a promotion, or trying to build a new business, these key questions can help you make it happen:

Who has the most to teach me about the success I'm after?
Who would benefit from my success once I have opened the doors I want to open?
Who is out there looking for an ally like me? How can I help someone else reach his or her goals as I reach mine?

Understanding the Culture

When I was heading into a new workplace years ago, an older businessman told me, "Remember, no matter how good you are at your job, at least half of how well you do will depend on politics." Another word for that kind of politics is culture. Office culture is all about whether you seem like a team player, and whether your personal success benefits others. Sales culture is similar, only more intense.

Here are some key questions to ask to understand the culture of the places you work:

What are the personal goals of the other key people in this organization?

What are the personal goals of my sales prospects?
What kind of success are others here hoping I'll have?
Who are the most respected people in this organization, and
* why?*

Important: Don't fake it. If your goals don't fit, or if you don't respect the goals of others in the organization, look for another place to work. You can't fake the real commitment to helping others meet *their* goals that you'll need to master the culture of your workplace.

Building Success

Long-term success at work builds on the same foundation as opening the doors and understanding the culture. It all goes back to asking the level-three questions every day, as you encounter colleagues, prospects, bosses, and employees:

How do other people see themselves?
What are their goals for themselves?
How can I help them reach those goals?

9

THE POWER OF TEAMS

THE HOME TEAM

> *The critical questions for making your family work as a team are the same as making teams succeed at work: How do my spouse, my kids, my siblings, and my parents see themselves? What are their goals? What can I do today—and in the long run—to help them reach their goals?*

At home, you start out as part of a team without even trying. If your family worked well as a team when you were a child, you probably absorbed many of the values and skills that you need to make your family work as a team now that you're an adult. If your family wasn't a strong team when you were young, you'll probably have to be much more deliberate and thoughtful in making your new family succeed.

The critical questions for making your family work as a team are the same as making teams succeed at work:

How do my spouse, my kids, my siblings, and my parents see themselves?
What are their goals?
What can I do today—and in the long run—to help them reach their goals?

Perhaps the hardest thing about being a parent is that our children need to grow into people we sometimes can't even imagine. Two students of mine come to mind. One was a young man from Iowa, with bright red hair, a face full of freckles, and a ready smile. He was a student in a freshman English class I was teaching at Harvard University, and late one evening I bumped into him as I walked across campus. He was coming out of the library with a stack of books under his arm. We said hello, and I asked him how things were going. This was no simple question a few weeks into his very first term at such a daunting institution. Some of my first-year students were already showing signs of serious stress. Most would find their balance, but some would ship home, often because Harvard really wasn't a good fit. But this young man was a special case. He was having a great time, he told me. In fact, he was happier than he had been for years. He was so thrilled to be among so many people with so many incredible interests and talents. He tried to explain why this was such a big deal to him. He was a humble young person, not at all a braggart, but he was obviously one of the incredibly bright Harvard kids that many faculty, myself certainly included, quickly understood were smarter than we were. This sweet young man was one of the elite of the elite when it came to raw brain power. His parents seemed to have done a great job—not only was he screamingly smart, he was nice. But, he told me, he had never fit in in his small hometown. From the time he was about ten, he was years ahead of all the other students in his school. His teachers and his parents struggled to keep up with him. He was a genius growing up in a little farm town, part of a family that loved him, but barely understood him. How can parents raise such a child? How can they help him get to where he needs to go when that destination is such a foreign place to them?

The answer is questions. Asking what the genius son was thinking about, asking him to share the lessons he learned, letting him talk and teach and dream out loud. And it turns out that even regular old kids need exactly the same treatment much of the time. Another student I recall vividly was a young man I met while I was teaching at Parsons School of Design in New York, an art college that drew students who dreamed of becoming painters and graphic artists and clothing designers. This particular student had long, spikey black hair (so black it was almost blue—not quite a natural color), long black-polished fingernails, and dark makeup around his eyes. He wasn't much of a conversationalist, but he loved his studies and was reputed to be an outstanding artist. I asked him once where he'd grown up. Given his style, I'd have guessed lower Manhattan or maybe Beverly Hills. "Omaha, Nebraska," he replied, and I must have missed a beat as I tried to frame a reply. "I know, I know," he said, "I was lucky to get out alive." Now, I've been to Omaha, and it's a lovely place. But I can't imagine that this spike-haired, make-up-wearing young man fit in there any better than the supergenius from Harvard fit in in his little farming community. In both cases, their parents helped them find perfect places to grow into adults and helped them grow into people who knew what they wanted. But this young man's parents also found him a little strange, even though they loved him without reservation. Even his mother had never worn as much makeup as he did. How could those parents guide their son to a place totally foreign to them? By asking those important questions. By listening to his answers. By making it feel safe for him to dream.

THE HOME TEAM PART TWO: SHOWING UP

"Eighty percent of success is showing up"—*Woody Allen*

It's easy to forget that much of family life is about the very undramatic moments of being together, even if nothing particularly profound or loving seems to be happening. In my life as a parent, I have a lot of memories of those major events— graduations, home runs, first days of school—and a few, too, of those quiet moments of conversation when I felt I could see my kids turning into adults right before my eyes. Maybe the biggest lesson when I think over all those moments is how small my role in the drama has been. Being a part of a family that works as a team is not about the hero moments. It's not about making bold plans and getting the rest of the crew to fall in and execute them. It's not about *me* at all. That might be the very best lesson of family life—the humility it takes to be a good parent, the way that you need to support everyone else, and let your hero self fade, so that your family self can do the work of supporting the people you care most about as *they* become the heroes of their own lives. This is not easy stuff to do, and not easy to figure out. At least it wasn't for me.

The lessons in the humility of family life began for me in a big way when our first child was born, while I was in graduate school. Of the classes I was taking back then, my favorite dealt with Henry David Thoreau, remembered today for walking away from "civilized" life and going off to live in the woods. Many scholars have pointed out that Thoreau's cabin, built and celebrated in his book *Walden,* was hardly isolated—he remained within walking distance of Concord's town center and regularly walked to the homes of friends and family for hot meals—and so his claim to be throwing off the comforts of civilization was a bit overblown. Still, I was tremendously drawn to the very idea of what Thoreau had done—to live deliberately, as he wrote, without any unwanted compromise with society. Struggling as I was to make my way through graduate school, earn money, and be a good husband and father, the notion of throwing it all over and walking off into the woods to live by my own compass was enticing.

Early in *Walden,* Thoreau wrote: "Most men, even in this comparatively free country, through mere ignorance and mistake, are so occupied with the facetious cares and superfluously coarse labors of life that its finer fruits cannot be plucked by them." This struck a chord. As a happy dad but a tired one, I could see what he meant. But would taking up a solitary outpost in the woods tutor my soul in a way that the company of my wife and baby daughter could not? I had trouble believing that. Most days began for me with my wife waking me at about seven, as she dressed for work and headed out. My year-old daughter woke a bit later, and we'd have breakfast. Then we'd bundle up and head for a nearby park to play for an hour or so.

The park was a classic city spot—no grass, lots of concrete, a fierce steel jungle gym, and a sandbox bearing more resemblance to kitty litter than beach. There was another father I'd see every so often, a man who had completed a PhD in Russian literature at Columbia, then spent years making a living painting houses. He had finally settled into a career in public-health research, working mostly from home. He knew Thoreau forward and backward, and we enjoyed talking about books. Eventually, a couple of moms joined our circle, and every few days I could look forward to engaging book talk at the playground.

Sooner or later, I asked nearly everyone I met in those days what I called "the Thoreau question." Thoreau had summed up his goals at Walden Pond with these words: "I went to the woods because I wished to live deliberately, to confront only the essential facts of life. . . . I wanted to live deep and suck out all the marrow of life." My question was this: How would *you* go about living deliberately and confronting only the essential facts of life?

The Russian literature expert stood with me on a cool fall day as his three-year-old son wrote his name again and again on the park's concrete floor and my daughter plucked the last petals of October flowers growing nearby. "I *am* living deliberately," he said. "I love Thoreau, but I resent his implication that a man like me—living with my wife and my son as part of a family, going to work because I need the paycheck, going to the supermarket because the family needs food—that I'm a victim, that I'm a conformist. I know I'm making compromises day to day, but that's only because my ambitions are greater than

Thoreau's were. Or not greater, maybe more connected. I'm part of a family, and he was not. That's a choice I make every day; it's deliberate, and it gives my life meaning. I couldn't live alone on the edge of a pond without my family. That would *not* be sucking the marrow out of life for me; that would be hiding from my destiny. It would be a kind of exile."

"An exile from what? Your family?" I asked.

"Well, yes, but more than that. An exile from my public life as a father. I like being known around here as Daniel's father."

"Is that enough for you? You don't want more?"

"I do want more, but not the way Thoreau wanted more. I want more ordinary things, not more self-indulgence. You know, Thoreau talks now and then about Eastern philosophy. Do you know what I think the most transcendent Zen approach to life is today? It's a guy wearing a white shirt and tie, working at a desk, conforming to ordinary life with joy because he's living the life that others live. To find transcendence in the ordinary is the highest spiritual place to be. The ordinary isn't just the fish in the pond and the bugs on the ground that Thoreau writes about. The ordinary is what mothers do when they feed their kids. It's walking the dog and living a domestic life with joy. That's as rich and original as going off by yourself for two years, I think."

One of the young mothers at the park, part of our informal book group, had a different take on things. "For you," she said to my friend, "maybe that's true, because you're not just doing what you're told, right? You're breaking the mold by being home with your boy during the day. That's not what most men do, but you're doing it. It's different; it's more meaningful. But what if you were doing only what you were expected to do?

What if you were being exactly what everyone in the world said you should be, and you had no sign of original thinking in anything you did?"

It was a powerful question, in part because of what we knew about this woman, the wife of a lawyer who worked long hours and expected her to take care of their daughter without a thought for life beyond the playground. "Well," I asked her, "what's *your* answer to that question? Are you saying that there's something wrong, or something missing, from what you're doing with your life right now?"

"No. I'm trying to say that what I do today is particularly hard for me because it has nothing to do with who I want to be. It's not a statement. It's not a lifestyle. It's a commitment to Sue," she said, looking at the little girl she was holding on her hip even as she calmly explained to us how limited our outlook was. "Thoreau's problem is that he can't see beyond himself. I think you two guys have the same problem—it's like you're watching yourself in a movie, being the hero, the Lonely Guy at Walden Pond, or the Good Dad in the park, or the Suffering Husband when you're cooking and cleaning and getting a taste of life at home. But it's not about you."

It was a beautiful day with a clear blue sky and very little street traffic to distract us from our conversation and the loveliness of being outside with our children. Her words brought us right back to where we were. She helped us pay attention to what we were doing, rather than the abstract notion of what it all meant.

"It means so much to be a parent," she continued. "But it's all about the child, and about what you do today to help that child. When you push harder, and try to make it mean more, you lose a lot. I have plenty of ambitions, and maybe I should have spent today working on my investment portfolio or writing an opera, but I didn't; I spent it with Sue because she's the 'finer fruit'—she's the reward. There's no such thing as living deliberately if you are part of a family."

"Really?" said my friend. "No such thing? I'm not living deliberately?"

"You play your part, and if you do it well, you do it with dignity and love. But it's not deliberate in the way I think Thoreau means. It's not all about what you want this minute. You became a better person by *not* living deliberately every minute. You have to give that up to live with other people, or at least to live with real regard for other people. I think that's the thing that Thoreau is missing. He's missing regard for other people. He's missing love. That's the price you pay for being all alone in the woods."

Then we sat with our kids, she opened a little bag of cream-filled cookies, and we enjoyed our own society under the blue sky, while I reflected on the lessons in humility my new friends had been teaching me that day. I still thought Thoreau was pretty terrific, but I knew that Sue's mother was right—that at the heart of his project of going off to live in the woods was a kind of selfishness that I could not afford if I was going to help my new little family become a team that worked for our kids, and for my wife and me. Solitude had its charms, but the higher purpose for me would be dedication to the needs of my children and my partnership with my wife. Maybe I would have thought brilliant thoughts if I had run off to a calm woodland cloister for a couple of years, like Thoreau. Maybe I might have written half a dozen books with all the time in the world for my efforts. But I know that the different path I followed, by showing up every day to play my supporting role in the life of my family, has been a much greater contribution to the world and helped me to become a better and happier man.

THE HEART OF ONE COMMUNITY

In one small town, a group of community activists tried to make change by fighting the merchants in their town— and failed. When they framed their problem in a new way, and emphasized the common goals they shared with the key merchants in town, they built lasting success.

Sometimes, when the stars align, we discover that we are less alone than we might think—that our neighbors are more than the people who live nearby, but people who share our values and commitments, too. One community in Connecticut rallied together to save a cherished community theater, revealing a town with a real common purpose, and a smart approach to keeping what they believed in alive.

The people in this little oceanfront town were almost desperate to save the theater when plans to shut it down and sell the building were announced. The theater, right in the center of town, not only represented a valued alternative to the big-chain megaplexes on the outskirts of town, but everyone feared what might become of the prime retail space the theater represented—maybe a low-end fast-food outlet? Maybe a couple of high-end boutiques that would add little to the fabric of the town center and alienate the less wealthy in town? A group got together and drafted a plan to keep the theater operating through a nonprofit community foundation, at a cost of about $600,000. Local residents figured they could raise about

$100,000. So where would the remaining half million come from?

A delegation of citizens approached a number of the merchants in the town center to ask for their help. Lots of goodwill, but relatively little money, came out of that effort. Most disappointing, the two largest businesses downtown, a major bookstore/café and an anchor store for a national casual-clothing chain, weren't willing to commit serious money.

Fortunately, someone among the community citizens group figured out the mistake they were making—asking the big retailers to invest money in the community group's goals. The better alternative, she realized, was to figure out what the retailers' goals were and find a way to help them reach those goals. At the high level, the retailers' goals were simple: to make money. But they had some important subsidiary goals, too—including, for the clothing store, plans to expand, which required community-board approval. With that insight in mind, the community group made a presentation to the bookstore/café manager and his regional VP, analyzing potential loss in sales if a competing store—a book shop, a café, a coffee shop, or a gift shop—took over the theater space. And they presented to the clothing shop, stressing the value that strong community support would have when the store went to the community board to seek permission for their planned expansion. In both cases, the local citizens were able to make their case in terms of the retailers' own goals. What they did was embrace the big merchants to form a single, larger team. The community group adopted the retailers' goals as their own, and in exchange they got the retailers to adopt the community group's goals. The end was a big win—they got the money they were after, and the theater is still open today.

THE POWER OF PURPOSE

STANLEY MILGRAM: THE IMPORTANCE OF STAYING CLOSE

Yale psychologist Stanley Milgram demonstrated that people are too easily influenced to do things they know to be wrong. The minority of the people he studied who were able to follow their own principles even under pressure had a few traits the rest of us should try to develop, too— they had practice explaining their core values to others, they were good at finding third alternatives when others presented them with black and white choices, and they paid attention to the personal experiences of others around them.

Getting people to work well in teams is crucial to accomplishing ambitious goals. Teams work a kind of magic in thinking important ideas and getting hard work done. But there's a dark side to teams, too; group identity can be too efficient, creating the power of groups at the cost of individual conscience and moral judgment. Perhaps the most important thinker about the dark side of group behavior since World War II was Yale psychologist Stanley Milgram.

In the 1950s, Milgram was thinking about ways to test human nature and human thought. He wanted to answer some fundamental questions about group behavior: How much are people controlled by authority figures? How are they influenced to do things they don't want to do or that they know are wrong? In the aftermath of World War II, he particularly wanted to understand how the large majority of the citizens of a modern nation were convinced either to participate in, or to be silent about, cruel changes in their culture.

In 1960 and 1961, Milgram set up his initial experiments at

a storefront in New Haven, Connecticut. People were recruited to work as experimental assistants, or so they were told. Men in lab coats posing as scientists said that the assistants were needed to help run experiments on people whose memory and learning abilities were being tested. But this was a ruse—in fact, the supposed subjects were actors, while the real subjects were the people hired to be the "assistants." The real question the experiments were actually trying to answer was, Would ordinary people be cruel—perhaps even to the point of killing—if an authority figure told them they had no choice?

The "assistants" were told that "learners" were in the next room, connected to devices that would deliver an electrical shock each time a learner failed to answer correctly a simple question read from a prepared list. Each time a learner got a question wrong, the assistant was supposed to pull a lever that delivered a shock, and then turn a knob that increased the level of the next shock. After a while, the learners began yelling in pain, saying they had bad hearts, yelling "you're killing me!" and eventually falling silent as the shocks continued (in most of Milgram's early experiments, the learners were actually recorded voices played on tape machines in the next room).

How many people would continue delivering the electrical shocks even though the learners clearly seemed to be suffering harm, perhaps even death? Which of the "assistants" would go on to deliver those shocks and which would at some point refuse, even though the men in the lab coats told them things like "You have no choice; you must continue" and "The experiment requires that you continue"?

I've seen the films Milgram made of those early experiments many times, and two insights continually leap out from them: first, even the people who continued to shock the learners all the way to the top of the scale seemed to be suffering—they knew what they were doing was wrong, but they seemed unable to resist the commands of the authority figures. They were not cruel; they were afraid.

Second, those who did find the ability to stop said things like "Of course I have a choice" and "I won't kill that man in there." These were people who were able to express their core values. I doubt those values were very different from the values of the people who ran the shocks all the way up. The difference seemed, instead, to be a self-awareness of those values, and some practice putting them into words.

Milgram's early experiments revealed some very important aspects of human behavior and made it clear that we need to re-mind ourselves of our own values time and time again if we are to have the strength to act upon them in critical situations.

As his early results were published, Milgram began per-forming new variations in his experiments. Among other changes, he experimented with changing the assistant's physical distance from the learner. In some experiments, Milgram required the assistant to take the learner's hand and place it on a metal plate for the shock to be felt. The results were clear: the closer the as-sistant was to the learner, the less likely he or she was to con-tinue to deliver the shocks. This is a major insight, and it should remind all of us of the value of human contact with the people who depend on us, upon whom we depend, and about whom we care.

Milgram's experiments are worth of a great deal of thought—they raise big questions about human society and the human heart. In addition to their social and philosophical value, they also offer some practical, positive insights, espe-cially about that idea of staying close.

Apply that idea to family life, and it suggests that regardless of the "quality" of time we spend with our spouses, children, and parents, there is no substitute for being in the same place at the same time, sitting next to the people we love, holding their hands, and simply being close. The application to business life is similar: if you want to do well in business, stay close to your employees, your customers, and your bosses.

Two Lessons from Stanley Milgram

People are more likely to do harm to others if they cannot express their own values, and if they don't remind themselves of those values often.

Getting close to others—being physically near them—makes it harder to do the wrong thing, so stick closely to the people you care most about, including your family, your neighbors, and your customers.

Keeping Close: Pay Attention to the People Who Matter Most

Two classic business stories reveal the unchanging fact: stay close and pay attention to the people who matter most, and good things will follow.

Inc. magazine columnist Norm Brodsky is a big fan of budget airline JetBlue and finds himself on their coast-to-coast flights often. On one recent trip, the silver-haired man whom Brodsky took to be the flight attendant introduced himself over the PA and said he would be going through the cabin to help passengers however he could—but he wasn't a flight attendant. He was Dave Neeleman, JetBlue's CEO. He worked the plane for the whole flight, meeting people, spreading goodwill, inspiring his employees, and gathering new ideas for customer service. Describing his encounter with JetBlue's boss, Brodsky wrote,

> I was sitting in the eleventh row, and it took him more than an hour to reach me. "Nice airline you have here," I said. "Where do you come up with all these great ideas—like the televisions [on all the seatbacks]?"
>
> "I get most of my ideas on flights like this one," Neeleman said. "The customers tell me what they want."
>
> "Oh, listening to your customers," I said. "What a novel idea!"

Brodsky might be surprised to see a connection between his encounter with CEO Neeleman and Stanley Milgram's experiments in obedience, but both reveal important truths about the humanizing effects of close contact between individuals, and the importance of breaking out of our group roles and identities at times.

Another classic business story illustrates the same point about sticking close to the most important people. It goes under the heading of "The Hawthorne Effect." In the late 1920s and early 1930s, a Harvard Business School professor named Elton Mayo conducted a series of studies at the Hawthorne plant of the Western Electric Corporation near Chicago. He and his colleagues found that the workers they studied benefited from improvements in their working conditions (like more break time and better lighting). No big surprise there. But they also found that the other workers in the plant—not the ones whose working conditions were improved, but the control group, those whose workplace had not changed at all—were happier and more productive at work, too. Why? Because they were being paid attention to—important men from Harvard came to visit regularly, study their work, and ask them how they felt. They performed better and became happier because they were getting more attention and had the regular experience of sitting in the same room with important people who cared about them and their work. The moral: pay attention, stay close, and good things will follow.

Recent research into bad behavior by teenagers has revealed that one of the most effective strategies parents can use to help keep their kids on track is to have family dinners at least three times a week. Parents don't have to lecture their kids during those dinners, or pray, or share horror stories about kids who break the rules in order for those dinners to have a positive effect on their teenagers' behavior. They just have to sit there and eat together. Even better if they share the kind of idle talk a bunch of strangers might—How are you? What did you do today? What are your plans for later? A teenager from Arizona offers a pretty accurate glimpse into why this is so effective: "Look, I do some things that I know I 'shouldn't' do, but I do them anyway, not all the time, and maybe not forever, but if I'm going to smoke and drink, I'm going to smoke and drink. Still, though, I usually wait till my parents are away, or at least if they're still around the house maybe I'll wait till I know they're going to be working on a project or something so I don't have to sit there and have dinner and all that and say, Yeah, I'm going to study with Jill later, and blah blah blah, when I know I'm going to go out and just drink. It really just kind of kills it if I have my mother's voice in my head all night from the stupid kitchen table while I'm trying to have fun."

So ten points for Mom, when taking time for a family dinner can kill her teenager daughter's plans to go out and drink all night. Just the fact of being close, of sitting for a while, looking at and listening to your family, helps people make better decisions and do more of what they know to be right.

The Three Elements of Successful Teams

What it takes for a team to thrive—common interests, common commitments, and common work that really needs doing.

The best definition of a team that I have come across is more than one person sharing common interests, common commitments, and common work. By this definition, the Green Bay Packers are certainly a team, and so is the ragtag group of fourth graders playing on the same side of a recess punchball game at PS 195. But this definition also allows some unexpected teams—like a husband and wife; the sales force at a manufacturing company; a group of neighbors working to clean up a vacant lot; and even a group from around the world connected by e-mail working to perfect the recipe for matzo-ball soup. All are teams because all share common interests (the desire to live a wonderful life together, to make more sales, to improve the neighborhood, to taste the perfect matzo ball), common commitments (ethical principles, belief in a larger goal—like a safer community for children or success for the company), and common work that needs doing.

Common interests are things that speak to all of us in the near term—they motivate us and they're easy to see or to imagine. Common commitments are deeper and driven more by values and long-term goals. Common work is clear enough—for a team to perform well, all its members need to see the clear and compelling work to be done that only a team can do well.

Teams missing any one of these three ingredients are likely to fail. In many cases, though, teams can be saved if you know which piece is missing and you can ask the right questions to start filling the gaps.

Here are number of questions and likely solutions for teams that are missing one of the three necessary elements.

Missing Piece	Critical Questions
Common Work	Without clear common work, is the team really necessary? Likely solution—Build a new team, starting with the clear work that needs doing, then find people who share commitments and interests to get the work done.
Common Commitments	Without common commitments, are the right people on the right team here? Likely solution—Swap people, create new teams clustering people who share the same values and long-term goals.
Common Interests	How can the short-term benefits of this team's work be shared among members? Likely solution—Create better incentives, communicate short-term advantages better.

Shared Commitments and Shared Interests

How to connect our values and beliefs to the work that needs doing—and answer that important question, why do we want what we want?

Shared commitments are the values and beliefs that motivate us, that help us explain to ourselves why we do what we do. Being of service to others can be a shared commitment. Raising healthy children can be a shared commitment. Shared commitments go beyond money, and beyond other short-term goals to answer that question, Why? Sure, our team wants to win, but why? Sure, we want to make money, but why? Many teams succeed in the short run because they have common interests—like making money—but don't last in the long run because the question of *why* was never really on the table. So long as the money chase held everyone's attention, this deficit of commitment wasn't that clear. Once the chase was over, the team was left asking, Now what? In the short run, shared interests and shared work can be enough to hold a team together, but in the long run, shared commitments are vital for keeping the bonds in place.

Many marriages lose their glue just when the hardest work seems to be done—financial security seems at hand, the kids are launched—and the years of reward instead of sacrifice begin. But if the spouses don't share common commitments, if they don't agree what money is *for* beyond paying the necessary bills, or how to use newly abundant free time once work loses its economic necessity, freedom from short-term needs can signal the end, not a renaissance, of a shared life.

At work, similar lessons are easy enough to see. Many companies are filled with the virtues of self-sacrifice and service when they're scrappy start-ups with nothing to lose. But the ones that thrive at the next level are the companies that figure out what comes next—what their missions need to be, beyond survival; what their model of service can be for the long run; what will replace the noble struggle to survive.

This lesson is all too vivid in community life as well. Many families that climb the economic ladder look back on their threadbare days wistfully. With less money, people tend to live closer to one another, to rely on one another for support like shared child care, swapped labor on home improvements, and shared open space for play. As income goes up and homes get larger, hired sitters replace neighbors who watch the kids; hired contractors replace the weekend gangs of neighbors sharing their labor, and private yards replace shared open space. The short-run needs for community collaboration fade. The economic incentives for community life lose their pull. What's left are the intentional aspects of community life—the groups that gather not because they have to, but because they share interests and values. Church groups become important. Political groups become important. Community groups built around a vision for the future rather than the struggle to get through the day become more important.

The people who find the most meaningful lives with growing prosperity are those who can tell you what they believe in beyond the day to day of life. Folks who can say, yes, this is where my passion lies, this is the vision I have for a better community, are the ones who make those better communities real. As daily life becomes more a matter of choice than of economic necessity, those who know where their commitments lie beyond the small interests of making it through the day and the week and the month are the ones who thrive.

The Third Ingredient for Teams—
What Is Shared Work?

*Real work gets real things done and leaves you feeling
like your labors have created something important.*

I grew up near the public beaches at Coney Island in Brooklyn,
New York. By the time I was twelve, friends and I would often
spend summer days down at the beach, mixing in with the
thousands of visitors from other neighborhoods. One day at the
beach a friend and I wound up arguing, about something trivial
I'm sure. He stomped off into the waves to drown his anger. I
stayed near the blanket we shared and worked my anger into the
sand, digging a deep hole. Then I glanced up and saw my friend's
new sneakers, sitting on the blanket. I looked at the hole. I
looked at the sneakers. In a flash, the sneakers were in the hole.
I shoved sand on top of them, and turned for home.

That night, my friend's father called my house and my own
father picked up the phone. "My son's shoes," my friend's father said, "are gone. I'm told that your boy took them. Do you
know where they are?" I eventually confessed. My friend's father asked to be paid for the cost of a new pair of sneakers.

But *my* father, very angry, had a better idea. He marched me
down to our basement and told me to grab two of the old iron
gardening shovels rusting in a corner. Then we went back upstairs and headed out the door. We were going to the beach.

I was embarrassed, and frightened. My father was capable
of real anger and expressed it without apology. But it was a
beautiful night, and we were walking under a sky full of stars to
the ocean. Now, the beach at Coney Island runs for about four

miles, and when that beach is empty and the surf hits the shore with all its noise in the quiet night, it seems even bigger. I had only a general sense of where my friend and I had been sitting. My father and I picked a likely spot and began to dig. After about an hour, I told my father I wanted to go home, that I'd pay for the sneakers myself, and that what we were doing was nuts. "Dig," he replied.

I dug. We dug. The night was cooling under the bright stars. After a while, we talked a little bit, about the sand, the ocean, my rotten friend. It was a good night to be doing real physical labor with my father.

Then I hit a sneaker. It felt like striking oil—my dad and I were both thrilled. Another hour later my father dug up the other one about fifteen feet away. Do sands shift that much on summer days? We didn't know, but we walked back home like working men, tired and happy to be together.

That, in sum, is the value of shared work, something my father understood to be far more precious than the cost of a pair of new sneakers. Accomplishing something difficult, working like a team, and coming home tired are irreplaceable feelings—only real work can provide them.

Why Teams Fail

> *Understanding how teams can work well—with common commitments, common interests, and common work—is not quite the same as understanding how and why teams fail. Understanding these failures is critical, though, for learning how to fix broken teams. Here's a quick look at some typical teams in trouble and ways to fix what's broken.*

What Happens When Common Commitments Are Missing

In the community ... A block association forms to stop the building of a group of densely packed condos in a suburban area of large-lot, big-backyard homes. A number of the condos will be set aside for low- and middle-income residents. At the first block association meeting, several people talk about blocking the condos because they don't want poor people in the neighborhood. Others talk about the influx of new families adding enrollment and cost to the local school. Someone else makes the point that the town is running out of ball fields, and that this privately held open space should be bought by the town instead and made into a public park. If these folks try to take action too soon—before they talk about their different motives as well as their common ground—they'll probably do more harm than good.

This group needs more thinking and talking time before they start acting. Even though they all want the same thing—no condos—the team is vulnerable to smart opponents who will drive wedges into the team based on the different values within it. They need to ask themselves what they all agree on and shape a vision of their community's future that everyone believes in. Only with that common commitment can they become an effective team.

Best next steps: Have those hard conversations, find the real points of common agreement, and move forward with a united front.

At work ... A collaborative sales team is set up, but some members are totally focused on the short term. They try to maximize their commissions without considering the long-term value of accounts that start small but can grow much larger over time. This is a common problem in sales teams that emphasize short-term goals—teams in which people say "we've got to make the numbers" all the time without also setting and reaching measurable goals for building long-term success as well. A likely path for positive change in this situation is to tie sales bonuses to long-term financial performance and link significant compensation to the success of the team, as well as rewarding individual performance. Common commitments are all about the long term. When you see that they're missing, you know it's time to focus on the long term, to balance the short-term intensity that's important for success but not sufficient in itself.

Best next steps: A leader has to emerge to help this team focus on the long term, whether that leader is the boss who oversees the team, or a member of the team who can rise to the occasion and help convince the others that he or she has a vision they should all buy into, to help them reach their own goals.

At home . . . A mother makes a plan for a college-visiting road trip with her teenage daughter and pays for a rigorous SAT-preparation program. But her daughter resists, complains about the trip for weeks, and then late one night shortly before they're supposed to leave, she tearfully confesses that she doesn't want to go to college at all. The mother's mistake was to assume that she and her daughter had the same long-term goal—college. But she might have been wrong. That doesn't mean that when her daughter sees all of her options clearly she won't want to go to college—it could simply mean that the daughter isn't sold on that plan yet.

Best next steps: Mom (and Dad, too, if at all possible) need to spend time thinking about college from their daughter's perspective. The parents need to understand why their daughter thinks college isn't for her, to correct any misperceptions and fill the gaps of missing information to help her get to the place where college will seem more exciting, or, failing that, to help her explore sound alternatives to college. But until everyone in this family stops taking common commitments for granted, and until they all start talking and listening about what they want in the long run, they're likely to spend too much time spinning their wheels and not enough moving forward.

What Happens When Common Work Is Missing

At work . . . Have you ever seen this at work—a new committee meets to figure out what they're expected to do? Obviously something is wrong here, because a team exists even though its mandate to get something specific done is pretty soft. This is an all too common situation. Someone higher up in the organization has created a team without really understanding what needs to get done. But the team knows enough not to protest, and they decide to create an advisory report for a senior manager who has not asked for one. That way they'll actually have something to show as an outcome of their work. Smart politics perhaps, but a genuine waste of time and talent. In a situation like this, where common work is missing from a team's mandate, it's best not to pretend. A smart boss will disband the committee and create new teams around common work that clearly needs doing.

At home . . . Make-work and fake work pop up at home, too. Picture this: Dad believes teen boys need to be kept busy; he gets his two sons out into the yard early Saturday morning to mow the lawn, though the grass is already too short. A productive solution isn't hard to find. Dad can work with the boys to decide how their time, talent, and effort can best make a positive difference for the family or community. He can use their own energy and insight to help them—and himself—learn about the difference between merely putting out effort and actually getting things done.

In the community . . . A community support committee is organized by a group of neighbors who want to make more of a contribution to the overall well-being of their town. They decide to raise funds for a local hospital by selling sponsorships for a community newsletter. After a while, more than one committee member realizes that they're investing thousands of dollars of their time in order to raise hundreds for the hospital. Some committee members choose to skip selling the ads prospect by prospect and just write checks. Remember: the process of teamwork should have value in itself. Busy work is a weak foundation to build upon—better for these folks to donate money instead of doing low-wage selling work, and then donate their time to work on tasks that are more personal than selling ads, like visiting patients in the hospital they're supporting.

Key insight: There's always real work to be done. Use the power of the team to find it. Don't fracture the team with fake work.

What Happens When Common Interests Are Missing

Teams that fail because they lack common interests—the short-term payoffs of group work—are some of the easiest to fix.

At home . . . Picture this: a family's annual week of vacation in the mountains is coming up, but Dad has a Habitat for

Humanity project he wants to stay home to finish, Mom wants to skip out for a day to meet with a client, and each of the kids has either a key game with a sports team or a big concert to perform in.

Everyone's mad at everyone else for their lack of commitment to the family's traditional week away. This problem is a classic case of absent shared interests: everybody feels they'll gain more by doing something else.

The only solution: this is the wrong week for the big trip. But this family does still have strong shared commitments—their commitment to the family is key. So, in exchange for everyone getting a free pass this time, all have to agree to a new week a few months out and promise not to schedule in any conflicts, no matter how important. They need to express their common commitments by arranging for some common interests, if not this particular week, then for a week in the future. A liberal attitude in excusing everyone this time will have to be balanced by a tough "no-excuses" policy next time, and everyone needs lots of fair warning about this.

At work . . . Here's a team that needs to be fixed: the senior managers of several different divisions work together to make policy decisions for their parent company, but bickering and harmful political jockeying often derail good plans. Why do they fight with one another? Sure, there are some specific grounds of disagreement among them, like the locations of key meetings and who has to do what homework, but the deeper answer is that their group work is badly structured—the little disagreements loom large because there's more to gain for each individual by fighting the little things than there is by agreeing on the big things. When there's more fighting than agreeing—and when the focus is on details instead of principles—you've got some big clues that the incentives for group agreement and success aren't clear enough.

The clear need: the big boss—likely a chief operating officer or CEO—must change the relationship between the divisions and the larger whole. Structures that reward the individual divisions for other divisions' success are essential if this kind of cross-division team is going to do any good. Two executives in this group fight over whether the next corporate meeting will be in Miami or Las Vegas. Why the fight? One lives near Miami, and the other, you guessed it, lives near Las Vegas. So there's some short-term advantage at stake here. Until the leader of this group can answer this question—what do these folks gain by agreeing that's worth more to them than the cost of being away from home for a few days?—the fighting won't end.

In the community . . . Consider this case, in which the town pool is running out of money just as the summer's heating up. Community members form a support committee and agree to staff the three positions at the pool (excluding the professional work of the lifeguard—the volunteers will unlock and lock up, check IDs, and run the snack bar).

But after three weeks of the new plan, everyone's exhausted. One lady wants to scale back her involvement to only the days her teenage daughter spends at the pool, so she can keep an eye on her. Another key player wants to work only in the early morning, so he can grab a few minutes of having the pool to himself before he unlocks the gate and lets the public in.

As a general rule, the likely success of teams decreases as the size of the team increases. But this case is an interesting exception. This is one of those few situations where a bigger team can have a positive impact, because the ability for people to have a positive impact in this case is cumulative—more people with more time means it might be OK to let people focus on interests that aren't shared across the group.

Key insight: Putting all your cards on the table—and creating an atmosphere that encourages others to do the same—helps sort out straightforward answers to the "what's in it for me" questions that everyone thinks about at times, even if they don't always ask them out loud.

When you reach the conclusion that a team is failing because it's missing common interests, you've got to get to the sometimes crass level of specific rewards for team members—the "what's in it for me" question.

Teams need all three legs of the stool in order to stand—they need common commitments, those bedrock values and beliefs that help us stay focused on what we see as right; common work that really needs doing; and common interests, those short-term benefits that reward all the players and help them meet their personal goals.

10

HOW TO BE A TRUTH TELLER

> *A kind approach, a humble attitude, and careful atten-*
> *tion to the good among your opponent's positions will al-*
> *ways carry your further in argument than the foolish*
> *assumption that you represent the right and your oppo-*
> *nent the wrong.*

Probably the greatest American persuader was Abraham Lincoln. History remembers his leadership in the Civil War as his
greatest contribution to the nation, but his letters and speeches

are a remarkable set of documents, charting paths in moral argument that few others have ever equaled.

Perhaps most significant in Lincoln's arguments was not the substance of what he had to say—though that substance was tremendously important, leading to the end of human slavery in our country—but his skill in saying it.

One of his most interesting speeches was on February 22, 1842, to a temperance group—a group of citizens in Illinois trying to ban alcohol. In addition to applauding their cause (though he himself took a drink now and then), Lincoln spent some time in this speech to describe his methods of argument.

"When the conduct of men is designed to be influenced, *persuasion,* kind, unassuming persuasion should ever be adopted," he told his audience. Why? Because it works, yes, but also because Lincoln feels that though he is *right,* he is not *better* than his opponents. He is speaking specifically of temperance when he says, "In my judgment, such of us as have never fallen victim have been spared more from the absence of appetite than from any mental or moral superiority over those who have." Yet he seems to feel this as a general point, beyond the question of drink. Those who are wrong are not inferior—simply mistaken and misguided. They can be converted to the right as Lincoln sees the right.

In a later speech arguing against slavery—hitting hard and making the moral case that the practice at the center of the Southern economy is simply wrong—he turns directly to Southern slaveholders and tells them, capturing the very heart of his moral and rhetorical approach, "this is not the taunt of enemies, but the warning of friends." That is, he is not rejecting them as people, not refusing any common ground, but instead trying to build *more* common ground, trying to find those common commitments that will save them all from the disaster of all-out war.

Though Lincoln's art and craft as a speaker were not great enough to prevent war, they were great enough, at least, to bring the institution of slavery to an end, and to create a framework for a lasting peace and an enduring American nation. Surely there are lessons to be learned from his approach to making a good case clearly and well.

On October 16, 1854, Abraham Lincoln gave a speech at Peoria, Illinois, in which he asked a direct question to the political leaders of the Southern slaveholding class. "In 1820," he wrote, speaking of the national policy to outlaw the slave trade that had enjoyed broad support in Congress, "you joined the north, almost unanimously, in declaring the African slave trade piracy, and in annexing to it the punishment of death. Why did you do this? If you did not feel that it was wrong, why did you join in providing that men should be hung for it?" That's quite a question to ask in a heated debate—"why did you do this?" It conveys the habit at the heart of Lincoln's power as a speaker— a genuine curiosity about, and empathy for, the motives of his opponents. And beyond that curiosity and that empathy is a kernel of faith in the decency of even those who seem ugliest and most dangerous.

Later in the Peoria speech, Lincoln adds a number of further questions about the souls of slaveholders. Specifically, he points to the large number of free African Americans at that moment in American history—a number he puts at 433,643, with precision that demands to be taken seriously. "At $500 a head," he tells his audience, "they are worth over two hundred millions of dollars. How comes this vast amount of property to be running about without owners?" Perhaps his listeners bristled at Lincoln's colliding the images of free men and women with their potential status as "property." Surely this is something of a trick, an assault on the ears and imaginations of his audience, a making bald and plain the fact that slavery as an institution demeans these hundreds of thousands of men and women so thoroughly. But he does not pursue this. Instead, he turns to the spark of something good inside the slaveholders:

> All these free blacks are the descendants of slaves, or have been slaves themselves, and they would be slaves now, but for SOMETHING which has operated on their white owners, inducing them, at vast pecuniary sacrifices, to liberate them. What is that SOME-THING? Is there any mistaking it? In all these cases it is your sense of justice, and human sympathy, continually telling you, that the poor negro has some natural right to himself—that those who deny it, and make mere merchandise of him, deserve kickings, contempt and death.

Lincoln's hope for the end of slavery—his hope for his nation's prospects of living up to its high ideals and purpose of human freedom—rests not in the strength of those who would force change on the worst offenders against the American ideal, but in the spark of goodness in those offenders. The free black men and women of his age are the physical signs and symbols of hope, and their freedom is testimony to the goodness that lives even in the slaveholding class. That *something* Lincoln speaks of is a thing he believes in deeply, and throughout his political career, Lincoln finds it in every opponent and enemy he faces. He argues from faith in those whom he opposes, faith that they will make the journey from wrong to right. And there could hardly be a stronger path to victory in American politics and statecraft.

In 1854, Lincoln also wrote a "fragment," a sketch of ideas later found in his papers, about slavery. Scholar Andrew Delbanco has pointed to this as a particularly important sign of Lincoln's modern sensibility about the nature of race. "If A. can prove, however conclusively, that he has a right to enslave B.," it begins, "why may not B. snatch the same argument, and prove equally, that he may enslave A.?——." In characteristic fashion, Lincoln next takes the side of his opponent: "You say A. is white, and B. is black. It is *color* then; the lighter having the right to enslave the darker? Take care. By this rule, you are to be slave to the first man you meet, with a fairer skin than your own." Note that Lincoln's use of the word *you* is pivotal here. This fragment never, that we know of, became part of a speech or letter; the best image we can conjure of Lincoln writing these words is the man at his desk over candlelight, with his opponents in mind. The danger of a bad argument, Lincoln reveals, is greatest to the man or woman making it. A weak argument might in fact lead to the doom of the person making the argument.

And so Lincoln comes to the aid of the slave by coming to the aid of the slaveholder, or his apologist, warning that to think poorly is to put one's own liberty at risk, as indeed it puts at risk the great experiment of liberty that, for Lincoln, *is* the United States. Lincoln continues, conceding to his opponent an attempt at clarification:

> You do not mean *color* exactly?——You mean the whites are *intellectually* the superiors of the blacks, and therefore have the right to enslave them? Take care again.

197

By this rule, you are to be slave to the first man you meet, with an intellect superior to your own.

But, you say, it is a question of *interest;* and, if you can make it your *interest,* you have the right to enslave another. Very well. And if he can make it his interest, he has the right to enslave you.

Lincoln's opponent begins here standing on logic, but should that logic fail he ends in chains. Lincoln's argument against him becomes an argument for him. His message is not "cede me my victory," but "let me save you."

TWO LESSONS FROM ABRAHAM LINCOLN

Seek common ground when you make an argument—tell your opponents, "this is not the taunt of enemies, but the warning of friends."

"Kind, unassuming persuasion should ever be adopted"—never seek to prove yourself superior, but always seek to learn from your opponent, even as you defeat his argument.

PLATO'S ALLEGORY OF THE CAVE: HOW (NOT) TO BE A TRUTH TELLER

When you know you're right, resist the temptation to stand up and declare the truth flat out to the fools who don't yet see it—find the opportunity to influence others by inching them away from their illusions instead.

A crucial building block of modern Western culture is the work of Plato—work that seems strikingly modern, though Plato wrote about twenty-five hundred years ago, and on the other side of the world. In Plato's important dialogue about government and justice, *The Republic,* he tells a story that scholars call the "Allegory of the Cave." The problem he describes sounds a lot like the problem of generations of Americans lulled into passivity by television and other cheap entertainments.

In Plato's allegory, he describes a world in which people sit inside a cave, never venturing out, watching images projected on the cave's back wall all day long. A large fire burns on a high ledge behind the people, and puppeteers stand in front of the flames with their puppets. The images on the cave wall that captivate everyone are about as close an equivalent to modern television as a man living in fifth century B.C. could imagine.

Plato asks, what would happen if a man were able to escape from this cave, and see the true sun rather than the reflected images of a fire? What if he were to see the rest of the world outside the cave, instead of only shadowed images? Well, Plato tells us, through his character Socrates, that man would go mad.

But what if somehow he managed to survive his raw encounter with the real, and then returned to the cave to tell the others about the unimaginably great world outside the cave— and about how pale an imitation of reality their sad cavebound existence truly is? What would happen? Plato tells us that this man would be killed by the others in the cave. They would not be able to stand the thought of living without their illusions.

There is a powerful glimpse of human nature in this story— in particular, the nature of the man or woman who does in fact know things that his or her peers don't know, things that could make everyone's life much better. You've seen people like this—maybe you've been one. You watch your children make simple mistakes, knowing how they could do things better. You see your boss or a colleague make a big mistake—zig where he should zag—while *you* know the better path. So what do you do? Most of us, like the doomed truth teller in Plato's allegory, want to rush in and say, Wait! You're doing it wrong! You're making a mistake, acting on myths instead of reality!

But Plato makes it clear: that doesn't work. Why not? Because it's self-centered. The message is not "Let me help." It's more like "I know better." The fact that you *do* know better is not the point. Remember, that's first-level thinking—it's about how you feel about yourself ("I'm right!"). At the second level, you might ask, How will they see and hear me as I try to change their minds? That's a better question to ask, but still won't do the job. The third level is where the potential for success really lies—the questions at that level are, What do these people think of themselves? What do they want, and how can I help them?

That suggests a powerful exercise, trying to figure out what the truth teller in Plato's cave could have done to convince his peers to turn around and consider what lies outside the cave.

Even in their debased state, the weakened, will-less cave-wall watchers do have some needs they understand, like the need for food and water. What if the truth teller began at that level, with a message like, there's better food and water—and more good things—out this door, outside the cave? What if the truth teller began by solving the problems his or her audience already knew they had, to build trust? Of course, this would be a longer process than just running into the cave screaming the bitter truth. Building trust takes time. But with this third-level approach—with the commitment to understand how others see themselves and how they understand their own needs—success is actually possible. Instead of ending up with a dead visionary, we might actually wind up with real change for everyone.

How to Be a Truth Teller

Have you ever stood in a supermarket and seen a parent yell at a small child? Chances are, the content of the parent's rant is entirely correct—adults do, generally, know important things children don't. But the blunt statement of the truth about what a child is doing wrong is likely to be about as effective as the truth teller's strategy in Plato's cave. The fact of being right does not matter half as much as the fact of communicating well, building trust, and demonstrating respect. The parent who can reach his or her child with a calm, caring voice—the third-level voice that builds on an understanding of how the child thinks and feels—is the parent who need not yell quite so often, and teaches empathy and effectiveness through example. The manager who understands what her employees want and need must seldom resort to the authority of the org chart or the paycheck. Taking a third-level approach, the smart manager doesn't scream the truth, but whispers messages that make others feel strong and successful. Only then are great change and real leadership possible.

FIVE LESSONS FROM PLATO

Much of what makes us happy in the short run is an illusion.

Demonstrating to others that what they believe is wrong can be dangerous.

You can't count on people to recognize the truth when they hear it.

People will fight to preserve their own ignorance.

You need a long-term, empathetic strategy to help people overcome their illusions.

Rehearsal Versus Real Understanding

Real power comes from genuine emotion and thoughtful understanding, not rehearsed speeches or faked feelings.

We all know people who are just bursting with insight—they can explain the underlying dynamics of any situation and can explain in five different ways everything you or I do wrong—but who don't use those insights to treat other people well. They're smart and full of knowledge, but just can't relate. And all their insights don't mean a hill of beans. They fail to reach many of their most important goals and miss the chance to help others. These folks are often doubly unhappy, smart as they are, because they can see how and why things happen—failed businesses, harmful family dynamics—but they don't have the skills to change them, because change comes through people, though relationships.

Many people who have poor relationship skills come across as stiff and unnatural, as though what they say is rehearsed instead of spontaneous. And plenty of people are actually taught the bad habit of rehearsing and performing conversation as a way of creating a false sense of confidence. But there's simply no substitute for the natural style of relating to others that grows from real insight and understanding. That's what distinguishes between the very best sales professionals, who always come across as insightful but natural, and those who seem to be too slick, or full of preplanned answers to every question. And of course children are experts at detecting and deflating insincerity. Offer a child you know ideas and words you've copied from others and see how quickly the kid makes it plain that you're not being real.

Relationship rehearsal is easy to spot. It's what happens when people focus on what they should say instead of on the ideas they want to communicate. When a salesman plans a sales call around key phrases, the call sounds stilted and artificial and has lots of blank places (asked questions they don't have a script to answer, what will they say?).

The classic example of rehearsal over understanding is the play *Cyrano de Bergerac,* written in the nineteenth century and taking place in Paris in the seventeenth. In the play, Cyrano, the hero, is madly in love with Roxanne, who in turn is dazzled by handsome Christian. Cyrano's nose is part of his problem—it's pretty big. But Cyrano is a poet, and a man with a gift for deep feelings. Christian enlists Cyrano to hide behind a bush, while Christian woos Roxanne, and feed him lines. Christian repeats Cyrano's moving declarations of true love. Roxanne hears Cyrano's words from Christian's mouth and falls madly for Christian. But Christian is not the man she thinks he is—whenever Cyrano isn't around, Christian comes off as a clod, and none of the soul that Roxanne truly loves is evident.

Far too many of us try to be like Christian—we try to look good and speak in impressive tones, but with words and ideas we copy from others. The real power in relationships comes from the kind of genuine emotion and understanding that Cyrano expressed. If we don't know what to say, we need to check our hearts and our minds to reflect on our true feelings and our ideas, not borrow other people's.

Many of the people who fail at relating to others fail because they are too much like Christian. Faced with a brilliant teacher, they learn only to repeat his words rather than understand the source of his passion.

THREE LESSONS FROM CYRANO DE BERGERAC

Short-term rewards are tempting—beauty and youth can sell with great initial power.

Long-term satisfaction comes from passion and commitment, not from the short-term virtues like beauty and youth.

The externals, like the specific words you use, can never make up for poor understanding or lack of belief in what you are doing or selling.

KEEPING IT REAL

Thinking at the third level can tempt you to tell other people what they want to hear without putting real thought and concern into your words. That's a temptation to resist.

We all love to be loved, but love—and praise and respect—can come too cheaply. Have you ever had the experience of having someone praise you, and feeling just wonderful, but then you see that same person praise someone else, someone you don't feel all that good about? It feels a bit like you've been fooled. The person who praises *everyone,* who lavishes grand judgments on all comers, cheapens the whole idea of praise. We all want to be appreciated, but the person who finds everything and everyone to be wonderful isn't really appreciating us at all. Genuine appreciation is about discernment, about seeing how one thing is different from another, and paying close attention to the true value of things. If the good words we hear from others don't reflect real thought on their part, they come to mean little.

Plenty of people are all too quick to praise; they cloud the air with words of delight even before they know who, exactly, they are praising. One of the great worries I have about people who give too much praise too easily is that they will balance that excess by being equally unreasonable in their anger. When we display strong feelings unconnected to careful thought, not only do we cheapen praise, but we make darker feelings too easy to express, too, I fear. Emotion becomes a kind of performance, tailored to the social display we conjure up for other people to witness, rather than expressing a balanced and thoughtful response to people around us.

In a way, expressing praise too easily is an easy trap for people working to operate at the third level of thinking. Tuning in to other people's goals and trying to understand how they look to themselves, we can too quickly see the chance to heap kind words on other people, letting them feel like they are our heroes, filling the holes we can see them struggling to fill. But that takes the easy way out—it uses the insight of third-level thinking to score fast and cheap victories and avoids the harder and more meaningful work of building real human connection. This is, perhaps, the hardest part of thinking at the third level: yes, we want to help others in their struggles, but we have to keep that help real, and not give into the temptation to score quick points without offering real thought and attention to the people we encounter. Just as we all love to be loved, we love to give love—and we become stronger by giving love. But it has to be real love, the kind that takes time and care to develop.

THE POWER OF PURPOSE

A LESSON FROM PROFESSOR BROWN

How flexible you can be in expressing your ideas reveals how deeply you understand them.

Twenty years ago I had the privilege of studying with a philosophy professor named Malcolm Brown at Brooklyn College. Professor Brown wasn't a particularly well-known scholar or teacher, but he was a warm person and a gifted communicator of serious ideas, especially one-on-one. At the time, I. F. Stone, a noted muckraking journalist then in his eighties, was writing and lecturing about Socrates—he'd made mastering Greek and reading all of Plato in the original his retirement project.

I'd somehow come upon two tickets for a talk Stone was giving in New York, and Professor Brown came along. The two of us sat among about five hundred people listening to the small, slow-moving, fuzzy-haired Stone talk about Plato and his teacher and literary hero, Socrates. I wish I could remember exactly what Stone said that night, but most of it is lost to memory. What I do remember vividly, though, is a question someone from the audience asked after the main talk. The questioner might have been a professor himself. He posed his question; Stone, who was quite hard of hearing, asked the man to repeat it. Which he then did, but from a different perspective, in different language. Professor Brown lit up, leaned over to me, and said, "That man is a great scholar." "You know him?" I asked. "No, no," he replied. "It's the way he rephrased his question, dressed the same idea in different clothes."

That moment has been a touchstone for me ever since. Professor Brown taught me a tremendous lesson—insight is not about what you know (though knowing a lot helps), but about how you dress your ideas up. How flexible you can be in expressing your ideas reveals how deeply you understand them.

Think, for example, about actors. They have to memorize their lines, but what happens when an actor forgets a line? A poor actor stumbles, because he's been concentrating on the words he has to say—the "clothes," the externals of the character he is playing. A better actor who truly understands his character just says what the character *would* say in a given circumstance. A better actor grasps the underlying idea, who and what the character really is, and so like the philosophical questioner of I. F. Stone, he can dress his ideas up in different clothes with no anxiety.

That is the difference between rehearsal and understanding. Understanding is the key to meeting your goals; rehearsal is a distraction, all about the surface but in the end a false source of confidence.

The salesperson who rehearses presentation language but neglects the underlying problems solved by what he or she is selling, who rehearses rebuttals to objections but can't hear the ideas being communicated in those objections, who has the patter but not a deep understanding of the buyer's needs and experience, simply can't be truly comfortable—can't relate well—with the prospect.

The student delivering a presentation in class who has a memorized script but can't dress his central ideas in new clothes when challenged might get an A for oratory but won't find the real benefits of education until the script falls away and the ease that comes from mastering his ideas replaces it.

The parent who struggles with the question "What will I

say?" when a son or daughter has a crisis misses the critical opportunity to connect, to listen, to provide the aid and comfort and strength that a child in crisis needs.

So how do you make that leap from rehearsal into ideas?

The first step is to learn to listen deeply and to ask honest questions. Remember the three levels of thinking. Getting to the third level—figuring out how other people view themselves and their own needs—is an express train to the world of ideas.

Rehearsal is the classic expression of level-two thinking ("How will others view me?"). It's technically useful but solves no problems (and can create new ones). Asking the big level-three questions—What's going on in other people's minds? What are *their* goals for *their* lives?—opens the door to new ideas and new perspectives on problems that can seem otherwise impossible to solve.

How to Be a Truth Teller

Listen deeply. Don't think about how you will reply until the person you're talking to has said all he or she wants to say.

Ask honest questions that reflect real curiosity (don't ask questions just to steer the conversation where you want it to go).

Don't worry about how you look or sound.

Don't be afraid to ask silly questions.

Ask whether you're getting it right as you listen. Summarize what you hear the person you're talking to say, and ask whether you're on track.

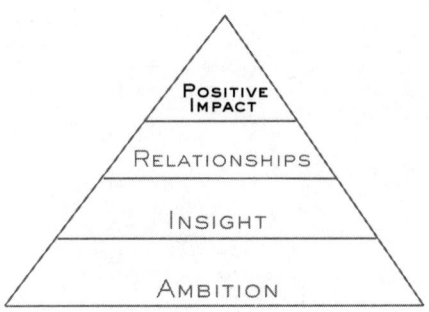

PART V

POSITIVE IMPACT: THE MOST WORTHY GOAL OF ANY HIGH ACHIEVER

When you've put all the pieces together—when your ambition is firing hard, your insights are cutting like a knife, and your relationships are golden—what's left for you to focus on? The answer is simple—having a Positive Impact on the world, the highest level of the pyramid, and the most worthy goal of any high achiever.

Wanting to make the world a better place is a cliché—but it's also the only desire that can really fulfill someone who has achieved his or her goals.

Remember Aristotle's most important observation—that happiness is not a psychological state, but a moral state. If you are unhappy, instead of trying to feel better, you should instead try to be better, to become a better person and to have a positive impact on others. Happiness will follow.

In more practical terms, I know for certain that achieving every goal without using your success to help other people is worse than staying on the couch and accomplishing nothing. Making the money you want and need, reaching the top of your game in your work and your play, building family relationships that feel great—this is all just the beginning. Making the lives of strangers better, making your town a better place to live, making our nation stronger and truer to its ideals—these are the positive impacts that complete the circle. They'll make you worthy of all the success you will achieve.

11

GIVING

BEING SUCCESSFUL IS ALL ABOUT HAVING A POSITIVE IMPACT on the world we share. How to have that positive impact? I can think of four ways—by sharing your time, your ideas, and your money, and by helping to build a common culture that brings people together.

WHY GIVE YOUR TIME? TO HELP OTHERS

> *Give to help others—and to be a witness to the world, to share the perspective of people who need help.*

Why give your time to have a positive impact? First and foremost, to provide value to others. But coming close behind that positive impact is the opportunity to witness parts of life that you might ordinarily overlook. It's almost a kind of personal ministry—putting your body next to people who suffer, people who need your help. It's a kind of testifying with your physical presence, witnessing the range of people's lives that extends well beyond your own.

The story of a friend of mine illustrates that point—but not in the way he would have wanted. This man had been a teacher for twenty years, but then left teaching to start a business that became very successful. His income more than tripled. At about the same time, he stopped picking up friends and family at the airport when they came to visit. "I can make five times what it costs to send a taxi to pick you up in the amount of time I'd have to spend driving to the airport and back," he'd say, "so why not have a taxi do the driving?" Fine economics, but kind of harsh in terms of personal relationships. The message my friend thought he was sending was, "I'm so generous, I'll pay for you to take a cab." The message others heard was, "I'm too important to come help you." There's no dollar amount you can attach to your time that can come close to that wonderful feeling of seeing a friendly face amid the crowd as you get off a plane. It's all about being there—putting your body where it can do the most good for people you care about. It's got nothing to do with money—the poor can do this just as well as the rich.

Every now and then we all need to shed the protections provided by our relative success—the distance from all kinds of unpleasant experiences that we can indulge in because of money, because of technology, and because of the fast pace of our lives and the press of obligations we all face. We need to do the simplest things in the world, to walk among our fellow citizens so that we see how they live. We need to know how it feels to stand where others stand. Of course, doing only this is not enough—we have to find other ways to help, too—but failing to do this is a great mistake, because our understanding of much of the world will then become secondhand understanding.

The trick is to find the balance between committing your time as a witness in a selfless way—and indulging in the feelings of involvement as a kind of selfish adventure. Standing in line to use a hammer for two minutes as part of helping to build housing for the poor is probably out of balance. Rushing to the scene of a disaster you see on TV so that you can express a personal need to help is probably out of balance. But walking through a poor neighborhood is not. Volunteering to visit older people who live without family is not. Volunteering to help children in low-performing schools is not. Putting your time in where others aren't already crowding around for the glory of being seen to help is the right way to go.

Committing for the long term to help—training as an EMT or as a teacher—is part of getting that balance right. Treating people who need your help with humility, with the knowledge that the best way to learn about them is to learn *from* them, is part of getting that balance right.

In the 1930s, New York business writer James Agee and photographer Walker Evans were assigned by a business magazine to travel to the South to write a report on the business of tenant farming, an occupation held by the poorest landless families and close to the life of the medieval serf. After a few weeks visiting among a number of families, Agee and Evans abandoned their original project, took leave from their jobs, and moved in with two families, sleeping on the floors of their shacks. Months later, they returned north without an article. The book they eventually published, *Let Us Now Praise Famous*

Men, is a jumble of images, descriptions, and ideas about how these poor families lived with dignity in a hard world. It is a book full of small, human-scale lessons about work, about family, about community, and about survival. It is full of humility and is one of the finest models of using time and physical presence as a form of witness.

Agee and Evans gave up on their outsiders' privileges in their roles as writer and photographer. Instead, they spent months simply living the lives of their subjects. Only then could they begin to write the kind of book they wanted to write—one that could convey a tiny fragment of the reality of tenant farmers, one truly about their subjects, and not about themselves.

The Trap of Looking Like a Hero (to Yourself)

Years ago, when I lived in New York City, I decided to volunteer for a well-known group that builds homes for the poor. It's a great model, getting people to invest their muscle and their labor in making the world better, and because the families who eventually will live in the homes work beside the volunteers, a wonderful sense of common purpose comes along with the common work.

As part of my efforts to lend a hand, I spent a day on a job site helping to renovate an old row house on the city's Lower East Side. I arrived early and began helping the handful of skilled tradesmen on the job set up for their day's work. I'd done some construction work in high school and by the standards I was used to, the worksite was a bit crowded and a little disorganized—pretty much what you'd expect from a group of volunteers with wide-ranging skills. But then around 9:30 the buses began pulling in. Volunteers from suburban churches got off and checked in. By noon, people were standing in line, waiting to use the hammers.

A couple of years later, I moved to a town north of Boston and called the local chapter of the same home-building group. They were working on a new project in the blue-collar town of Lynn and would welcome, they said, more volunteers at the site. While I was talking to the office manager about coming by to help out, I told her the story of my experience in New York. "Actually," she said, "we also have way too many unskilled volunteers. What we really need are people who can help us raise money, instead of more bodies out on the project site." They'd found that when people came out to work on a site, even if they did more harm than good while doing a day's work, those people would be more likely to contribute money, so they welcomed far more work-site labor than they really needed or could use. So I sent them a check and stayed away from the site.

The logic of this kind of participatory community involvement is wonderful—we all want to help, and we want that powerful third element of team-building, shared work. But unless that work is really needed, it tends to be more about us than about the people we're trying to help.

Instead of asking third-level questions—what do the people I want to help really need?—this kind of volunteering is stuck at the first level and revolves around the ways that we see ourselves as volunteers, instead of around the good we do for others.

As good as it feels to work all day knocking down walls for the sake of a poor family's future home, if that family needs $100 to pay a professional to do it right more than they need my particular help, once I subtract my selfish desire to see myself as a strong man who helps others (a level-one desire), there's no question that I can do more good by asking the people I want to help, "What is *your* greatest need?" and listening carefully to the response.

IDEAS: SOMETIMES THE MOST VALUABLE HELP YOU CAN OFFER

At times, the most valuable help you can offer others comes in the form of ideas that unlock opportunity.

Who has made the most positive impact on the world in the years you've been alive? Mother Teresa? An American president? The founder of Habitat for Humanity? Bill Gates? The answer, in my opinion, is none of the above. Instead, I think the obvious winner is Norman Borlaug, an agricultural scientist and winner of the Nobel Peace Prize in 1970 for his work in developing new strains of wheat and corn that could grow under harsh conditions, grow more food per acre, and grow with more harvest cycles each year.

While it is true that his work is today a magnet for controversy—Borlaug's innovations require "high inputs" of water and fertilizer and other ingredients scarce in many poor nations—Borlaug's work has made agriculture far more capable of feeding people throughout the developing world, and a common estimate of the lives his work has saved from starvation is more than one hundred million. Borlaug's contribution was not financial, not a great donation of his time, and not directly connected to the "glamour" charity work of giving out food to the poor or opening schools. But his ideas about how to improve plants did more good than any other human's efforts to help men and women on this planet in our lifetime.

Of course, most ideas that do good for others operate on a smaller scale. My father, Lloyd Temes, played a role in one such enterprise. Years ago, an engineering researcher named Mischa Schwartz had published a paper that included a chart that eliminated the need for some pretty difficult mathematical calculation necessary for diagnosing problems in certain kinds of sophisticated electrical machinery. Without that chart, only people with high-level math ability and training could fix these technical devices, including early computers. But with the chart in hand, a technician with limited training could do the work herself.

Much of my father's career was spent teaching at a community college, working with students who had barely squeezed through high school, and equipping them for well-paid careers as skilled technicians. He could do this—help literally thousands of people find meaningful and rewarding careers—because of Mischa Schwartz's chart.

What problems can you solve—in your home, in your community, around the world—with your ideas over time?

GIVING BY TEACHING

My father loved to teach in large part because he knew he was doing good by sharing his knowledge. He certainly did a lot of good for me. His most effective method for teaching me important lessons was mostly to get me in the car with him and drive. Driving was connected to talking with my father, reflecting his restlessness. Doing something—doing something *else*—helped distract him from his defenses, and looking out at traffic, devoting his tactical mind to the hazards of a hundred other drivers, he'd open other parts of his mind and at times his heart to me as I sat in the passenger seat.

I can remember a particular trip when I was about ten years old. I asked him, probably out of nowhere, how much it would cost to build a house. My father, an engineer, knew how much it cost to build a house. But instead of telling me the answer, he shared the question. He thought about it. Out loud. He began talking about how many rooms a house usually had—why people would want this many bedrooms, a big enough kitchen to eat in, a basement you could store your stuff in or use for parties. Then he talked about how big each room should probably be— you'd want a bedroom to fit the bed, but also to have some room for you to get up and walk over to the window, right? So you don't feel squeezed in a small space. Then he talked about what you'd need to build a house with all those rooms. How much wood would you need for the framing? He added together all the feet and then told me how much framing lumber costs per foot. Then he did the same with the flooring, the walls, the fix- tures, the paint, the siding, the windows, the doors, and on and on. Then we had a total cost for the stuff—but of course we'd have to pay for the labor. It must have taken close to an hour to walk through that imaginary house with my father, to hear him build that house in his mind, room by room, paying as he went, and doing a perfect job at it as far as I could tell.

All because I had asked a pretty simple question, How much does it cost to build a house? He taught me a few things with that answer. First, that this particular question—and, to a degree, all my questions—warranted serious thought. Second, that behind simple answers are complex processes (behind the statement "It would cost $100,000 to build a house" is a world of ideas and experience supporting that conclusion). And third, that complicated things can be broken down into their parts and understood.

There were, alas, plenty of times when my father didn't take my questions quite as seriously—times when I lacked the wisdom to ask them in the car, on long trips. But often enough, I'd ask a question and he would answer with some real thought. My mother, too, though she was less the engineer and less likely to pack as much mechanical detail into her conversations, took my questions seriously most of the time. Both of my parents talked to me in big chunks of ideas—in sentences and paragraphs. They would explain, not always but often enough, how the things I asked about connected to other things, causes to effects, beginnings to middles to endings. They would explain, at least some of the time, why things were the way they were—why we'd be going to a certain place, why I couldn't have what I wanted in a particular moment, what would have to happen before I could get it. They gave me the respect implied by serious explanations and they showed me models of logic—and useful illogic, emotion driving some of their teachings as well ("We're not going because I'm just too tired. Why am I tired? I have no idea, but that's just the way it is." Compare that to simply saying "No. We're not going"). That respect and generosity of spirit is a big part of what separates the greatest teachers from the rest—and is a big part of what makes the best teaching a true act of service to others, a way of giving back.

We're all teachers in different ways, if not in classrooms,

then as parents, as neighbors, as friends. But how often do we hold ourselves up to these high standards of honesty and respect—to ask only *real* questions, and to listen hard for the genius of original thought from our children, our students, our friends? The moment when I knew all this was possible—when I discovered that being a teacher could be like conducting an orchestra, standing at the center of an invisible shower of powerful music—was in graduate school, when a young woman was saying something about nineteenth-century British literature around a seminar table, going on for quite some time. The professor, a dapper man of some years, fixed her in a steady gaze, her words at first fast and full of the passion of her ideas, then slowing as she looked into this man's eyes, seeing what might be patience or what might be annoyance as he let her go on, and on. Then she paused. I'm sure the whole room of doctoral students guessed as I did—he's going to show her up, make her feel a bit of a fool for going on so long, for being so in love with her own ideas. And then this wonderful professor— his name is John D. Rosenberg—said, "That was absolutely brilliant. Just wonderful. Let's all take a moment and just think about that." And I was surely not the only one in the room who was moved by that humble appreciation of a young person's new ideas. How wonderful it was in a competitive, even arrogant, environment to hear a learned man say such simple words and reveal that he had been listening so well to this young woman's ideas and courage. To me, Professor Rosenberg is a model for my professional life, and for my life as a parent, a husband, and a friend. I try to listen hard to find the wonder of what my children, my students, and my neighbors say—and I hear quite a bit.

Giving

Giving money has its pros and cons—the trick is to give with skill . . . and avoid blunders like the "curse of $100 million."

Several years ago, *Fortune* magazine published an article about the ways that the richest families pass down wealth from one generation to the next. To most people—certainly I remember feeling this when I read the article for the first time—this seems like a pretty easy problem to deal with. We should all be so lucky to have problems like these—how many millions to give to this child, how many to give to that one, how many millions to leave to our favorite schools, and how many to leave to other charities. But a close look at the effects of inherited wealth reveals that money can be a burden as much as a blessing, especially for people who do not struggle to earn it but come to their wealth through their families. Just pick up the newspaper or turn on the television—you'll see all the stories of heirs gone in the wrong direction. Lacking the need to work, many don't. Their appetites are not controlled by their wallets and expand to ugly and destructive proportions. And their sense of entitlement grows.

The *Fortune* article told some notable stories about next-generation wealth gone bad, but also pointed to a number of positive stories of families that had somehow figured out how to make the transfer of wealth—at least some of it—work. One wise and very wealthy man summed up his principles for helping his children and other young relatives. The trick, he said, is to give them enough to do anything, but not enough to do nothing. At the time, he figured that meant somewhere around half a million dollars. That's enough for a fool to spend down in a few years (or sooner), but also enough to allow an artist, for example, to dedicate himself to his art while still being able to provide his family with a decent home and education. It's enough for a lawyer to choose to teach third grade instead of practice corporate law without having to sell her house (unless it's a really expensive one mortgaged to the max). And it's enough to allow a dedicated scholar to live in the library forever, provided that his appetites are adjusted to meet what he can buy on the interest on the principal, a modest $25,000 a year.

It's enough capital to start a small business—but if the business fails, it's not enough to start the next one. It's enough to fund an education in law or medicine, but not to provide a life of leisure once school is over. Ask anyone on your street—that amount of money (maybe adjusted up a bit for inflation—the article was published in the early 1990s) is enough to change their lives if they've already set ordinary expectations for their personal comforts. It's enough, in short, to enable anyone to do anything and to appreciate their good fortune. But it's not enough to do nothing while the world spins around you, with others providing for your comfort.

And it is a wonderful model for using your personal success to have a positive impact. The wealthy woman or man who gives too much and creates a feeling of entitlement in others does not have a positive impact. Perhaps he or she feels good giving, but giving poorly can do more harm than good. And though the positive feelings that come from giving are wonderful and important, they are not the point—the point is helping others.

Giving

* * *

Perhaps the greatest calculation in the history of giving was made not all that long ago by Bill Gates and his colleagues at the Gates Foundation. Since the foundation got into the business of giving away money it has donated more than four billion dollars specifically to global health projects, many of them centering around distributing vaccines. That emphasis on vaccines reveals the same kind of sharp logic that helped Gates build Microsoft into the biggest business success story of the twentieth century. I picture Gates and his wife, Melinda, thinking through a series of questions about how best to use their spare billions (the current endowment of their foundation today stands at about $30 billion) and getting to this central query: how can we do the most good for the most people with each dollar we spend? Finding new cures for diseases could do a lot of good; so could spreading education around the poorest populations in the world, and the Gates Foundation sends plenty of money into both of these worthy endeavors. But a close study of suffering in the world reveals this: millions of people die every year from diseases that we—and by "we" I mean, mostly, the industrialized world—have already cured. Dollar for dollar, we can do more good for more people by getting those cures we've already invented out of the laboratories, beyond the cities and countries that have well-functioning health systems, and bringing them down the dirt roads and over the mountain passes that lead to the vast population of poor people living lives largely unplugged from the industrial world.

And that's what the Gates Foundation has put, literally, billions of dollars into. They have spent billions taking vaccines down those dirt roads and have saved millions of lives. Their philanthropy isn't the flashiest, doesn't get celebrated as much, dollar for dollar, as any number of more glamorous ways of giving away big dollars, but it certainly has done an enormous amount for an almost uncountably large number of otherwise forgotten men and women.

Give to *This* School or Give to *That* One?

> *Having a positive impact is not about who has the most to give, but who gives it wisely and well.*

I believe in higher education and have dedicated many years of my life to university work. And I'm a graduate of two wonderful universities—Columbia University, where I did my graduate work, and the State University of New York, where I earned my undergraduate degree. Honestly, I loved Columbia every minute I was there. I felt it was a great privilege to study on that campus, with that faculty, and I got more than I gave in my years there. The State University of New York is a very different kind of place, without the centuries of tradition, without the star faculty, and without many of the facilities and resources of Columbia. Being there did not feel as special, though many wonderful things happened to me there, and I was fortunate to study with a number of very fine professors.

Columbia is brilliant in reaching out to its alumni. When I give them money, they make me feel special, a member of a wonderful club. SUNY has few fund-raising people on its staff, and they simply can't come close to creating the good feelings in me as an alum that Columbia does. But I swore early on that I'd always give more to SUNY than to Columbia, because SUNY needs the money more, and the core of what they do—taking working-class kids and turning them into empowered professionals—is more important in my book than the fine work that Columbia does in educating a group of students already in the elite. I could give a million dollars to Columbia and have minimal impact there (they measure their endowment in the billions). Or I could give a few thousand to SUNY and provide one poor student with a year of education—something of potentially world-altering significance. The point is that positive impact is not about how many dollars you give, it's how those dollars express your values. In my case, giving to SUNY is a commitment to my values about helping poor people rise up through education. My neighbor might say that his values are better expressed by serving world-class research into AIDS prevention at Columbia's School of Public Health, and I would never argue with him—he's just as right as I am.

The man who said that he wanted to give his children enough money to do anything, but not to do nothing, had a clear sense of his personal values and a brilliant ability to express them, whether or not they are the same values as yours.

You get to play the same game. The question to you, as you consider how reaching your goals will allow you to have a positive impact, is what change you want to help achieve in the world we share, and what values you wish to express through sharing your time, your ideas, and your money.

A CAUTIONARY TALE: THE CURSE OF $100 MILLION

How a generous gift in recognition of a great editor cost that editor his job.

A fellow I came to know and respect when I was head of the Great Books Foundation served for many years as the editor of an arts magazine, a publication that had enormous influence and impact in its field. He once rejected an article submitted by a woman he hadn't heard of—rejecting articles was a big part of his job—but she remained a fan. Upon her death, she left over $100 million to the magazine. That amazing act of generosity was at least in part because this woman believed in the work my friend had so successfully done for so many years with a small budget. Now, this magazine was not a for-profit enterprise, and my friend did not in any sense own it. Instead, he reported to a board of directors. Many nonprofit boards are rather sleepy, particularly if they trust the day-to-day head of their organization. They often meet to enjoy some social time together and rubber-stamp the organization's policies and activities. But there's no louder wake-up call than $100 million. My friend's board began to meet more often, and to worry about the money. They knew my friend was a great editor, but could he manage money? He certainly didn't seem to be the type—he looked and acted more like an artist than an accountant. And a number of people on the board began to say that while a good editor isn't all that hard to find—they don't cost that much to hire, at least—good money managers are a more precious commodity. The upshot was that my friend lost his job because of the huge gift from a lady who loved his work. Certainly that was not the goal of the donor, but it was the ultimate effect of her donation.

How can you avoid your generosity being used in ways you don't intend? If you've got enough resources, you can do what a number of donors to institutions in crisis do—they create new foundations, specifically to support the crisis-ridden institutions they care about, but with much more control over their money. So instead of giving millions to school X, I might give millions to foundation Y, which exists to support school X if and only if it reaches certain goals and seems to be moving in a positive direction. Or I might make a donation directly to the institution I want to help but put specific restrictions on how it can be spent. Best of all, I might find a person in that organization I trust, and speak unofficially with him or her, to get advice on how I can target my giving to have the most impact, instead of just sending in money in response to the next appeal the organization sends me.

Once we see that having a positive impact is not about who has the most to give, but who gives it wisely and well, we begin to realize that everyone has the ability to have a positive impact regardless of how much money is in their pockets.

I once called a nonprofit group I had an interest in and invited its executive director out for lunch. I asked him what help he needed most. I assumed that he would realize I meant what help his organization needed most, but he replied by telling me that he had to be in two places at once that weekend—at a party on the ocean where he needed to help set things up and make sure the event went smoothly, and at home with his son while his wife was away on a vital errand for her job. So I offered to help manage the party for him. He got to stay home and be a hero to his son and his wife, and I got to go out to the ocean. Later he called me and told me that he really needed that break—he was beginning to feel that his work was taking too much time from his family and thinking twice about his job, but getting past that weekend's conflict helped him recommit to his work. So my small contribution of time seemed to have a real impact. And I still feel great about that organization, because they gave me the great gift of feeling like I made a difference. The trick was practicing third-level thinking—asking the right question, listening to the answer, and seeing things from the other guy's point of view. I could have just sent in a donation, but even if I'd sent more than I could afford to give, I doubt I'd have done more good than I did by helping this organization hold on to a talented leader.

THE GIFT OF A COMMON CULTURE

Modern lives are fragmented—we live here, work there, stray far from friends and family, and often find ourselves alone. Even when we're with people we care about, it's all too easy today for us to be isolated, sitting beside a friend but staring silently at a television, or a computer screen, or talking into a cell phone. But then there are those wonderful—and all too rare—moments when we all look up, when someone says something that catches all of our interest and gets us talking. We discover one another and connect in a way that everyone understands to be precious. This happened to me about a year ago on a commuter train late in the evening. A couple in their thirties were talking about a television show—one of the "reality" shows. They were loud enough that a dozen of us, random strangers heading from New York out to the distant suburbs, not only overheard but also, because we had all at least heard of the show and knew something about one or two of the personalities on it, began participating. In a couple of minutes, we were all talking and smiling, the barriers between us lowered a bit because instead of trying to jump over those barriers by focusing on one another, we had that television show to focus on, a common point of reference, a safe enough subject that allowed us all to share public space in personally meaningful ways. We got to talk to one another and learn about one another's ideas. *You think the winner of this reality TV show is kind of shallow? What makes someone shallow?* Quickly enough we got from the superficial—the television show—to the substantial, the ideas about the common culture we share, that sit right below the surface of the show. I felt lucky to be in the middle of that spontaneous bit of community, and I know everyone else around me felt the same way. We were all smiling, and not because the talk was itself so elevating. We were smiling because we discovered that this kind of public conversation, this kind of connection among strangers, could still happen, that we still had important things to say to one another, that a random group of strangers zipping through the night on a fast train to the suburbs actually cared about one another.

Did our common point of reference have to be television? Sometimes it seems that just about all we have in common comes out of that flickering little light box. As that conversation on the train began to quiet down, I actually asked the young woman next to me, who had been a happy participant in our television talk, whether there was any book we had all read that we would be able to talk about just as easily. "I mean, what would that be, the book we all know? Hemingway?" I'd gotten lucky—she loved Hemingway, and we got to talk about his book about Paris, *A Moveable Feast*, for another few miles.

Talking about books has seemed like one of the very best ways to help support the common culture that most of us crave—and in fact I made a living for a while at the Great Books Foundation helping to support thousands of book groups around the country striking little sparks of conversation and building little public spaces for real community and culture. It might seem that in a world with any number of serious problems, getting people together to read and talk about books and ideas is an almost trivial thing to do. But we live in a society in which poverty is less materially awful than ever—the poor have more food and better access to shelter than the poor in other times and places have ever had. But poverty is no less terrible, because it is, for so many, a sentence of alienation, of being exiled from the public spaces, the common conversations, and those innumerable small joys of shared culture and connection that many of us enjoy. And it is not only the poor who feel that alienation. For all the incredible technology of communication we have in our world today, we are still too lonely, still too isolated, and still find it harder than it should be to find meaningful ways to share our ideas, our concerns, and our lives. Like the people I found on that train, most of us need a point of focus, something to talk *about*, in order to create that common space. And not only does a good book to talk about help us connect, but a great book now and then adds wisdom to our lives.

I was looking forward to just that kind of wisdom one night as I flew in slow circles around Chicago, wondering whether I'd be in time for a meeting in a neighborhood near Chicago's South Side to talk about a wonderful old book. This book in particular, *Democracy in America*, was written by a young aristocrat from France in the 1830s. He'd come to the United States to study American prisons but became fascinated by the broad sweep of American culture and wrote what is today, almost one hundred and seventy years later, still one of the two or three most revealing books about life in our country. Why, Alexis de Tocqueville asked in his book, are Americans so restless, so uncomfortable slowing down? With all that we have, why are we so ready to risk it all for the hope of doing even better, gaining even more, with the next business deal, or the next job, or the next move to a new town? As I circled over O'Hare airport, on my way back to town from a meeting in another time zone, de Tocqueville made a lot of sense to me. I was moving pretty quickly myself.

The couple hosting our book discussion meeting was an engaging pair. He had been a law professor and for several years the provost at the University of Chicago. More recently, he'd been a temporary cabinet member to the president of the United States, keeping a particularly sensitive chair warm after the former secretary had left but before the next had been found. He still had the kind of presence that gave even strangers the urge to call him Mr. Secretary. His wife had been many things and was in transition from a senior position at the United Nations to whatever would come next—she hadn't decided exactly what.

Their home was a brick and stone town house near the university—the home they had owned for thirty years, since he had been a young professor and she was the new bride, also a new graduate and a new teacher in the Chicago public schools. Through the years and the moves from Chicago to Washington to New York and back again, she had insisted they keep the house, to be sure they'd return to the only place she wanted to be their home.

My job for the evening was to help lead a discussion about de Tocqueville in their home, along with three college students, two retired professors (one in biology, one in philosophy), a law professor turned scholar of Judaism, a bank president, two stay-at-home spouses, a wealthy attorney, a part-time English professor, a young woman from New York recently arrived in Chicago and looking for a job, an accountant, a man recently back from Eastern Europe where he was helping to organize schools, and two other people whose stories never made it to my end of the table.

My plane landed. I drove out to Hyde Park to join the discussion group. I'd missed the wine but was in time for part of the dessert and all of the conversation about de Tocqueville. His central argument in the piece we discussed was that Americans suffer a peculiar kind of melancholy as the price we pay for our constant striving. It rang true. It certainly described the restless path that had led me from my Brooklyn to the life I shared in Chicago with my family then, with perhaps too many steps in between; it described the wanderings of our hosts in Hyde Park and was true of most of the rest of their guests that night, including my friend Gary, who was at the table with us, a native of upstate New York who had found his way out of his small town with the navy in a submarine, only to have his life changed when he read *Walden* a decade later. Thoreau led him to life as an actor in Chicago and most recently a second (third? fourth?) career as an itinerant trainer of book discussion leaders, traveling thirty weeks a year to teach teachers and lawyers, bankers and bakers, housewives and homehusbands how to take up where Socrates left off.

Gary was a road warrior and not the only one in the room. My wife was there, too. Her story started in Hungary, wound through the Bronx, the suburbs of Westchester County, upstate New York, Boston, Connecticut, and, for the moment, Chicago. The three college students in the room had all spent the last year traveling—Thailand, Burma, North Africa, most of Europe. They had been perhaps the most restless of us all, at least in recent months.

What did we all have in common? More than that, given how lightly our roots all held the local soil and how randomly the forces of career, education, and pure chance had led us all to the same home that night, to be neighbors for that moment, what did we have at all?

Aside from our private lives, what was it that we had among us as a public life, a shared experience, a sustaining common possession that we might have called the culture of America? This was the very question that de Tocqueville returned to again and again in his book, and it was really a restatement of the three central questions I've always found in the Great Books—What is the good life? What do we owe our neighbors? What must we do in the face of injustice?

In Hyde Park that night, we did not answer these questions decisively, but we did sit together and hear what our neighbors thought about them. In fact, to sit and think together about these fundamental questions is to answer them through our very actions. It is to create a culture that thinks, a culture that draws the individual citizen into the collective process of choosing what is right.

The questions, in the end, are what we have to share with one another. Our answers to these questions will of course be different, every one of us having a personal sense of purpose, reflecting our upbringings and the teachings of our parents, our communities, and our churches. But by sharing what we think and feel and know, and by paying attention to the ways that our neighbors are different as well as the ways they are the same, we'll help to build that common culture that sustains us when times are hard and makes life even sweeter in good times.

When we talk and when we listen, when we discover what our neighbors care about and put effort into learning and caring about the same things, and finding the inevitable points of connection to the things we care about, too, we give a gift often more important than money. We give a richness of community that is, in fact, priceless.

12

WHERE DOES PURPOSE COME FROM?

THE DAYS ARE LONG, BUT THE YEARS ARE SHORT

There's a truism about raising children that I've loved ever since my first daughter was born: the days are long, but the years are short. It can be such a struggle to make it from morning till night with a small child needing so much attention, so much help, so much care. Yet you blink and your infant is off to college. The days can drag, but the years fly by. Keeping this idea in mind can help you make some difficult decisions.

For me, one of the hardest decisions I ever had to make was when my oldest daughter was just a year old. My wife had been home with her full time but had just gotten an incredible job offer with a high-profile business magazine in New York, and she was ready to go back to work. I was in graduate school full time and teaching here and there. I could pick up some of the slack, but not all. We needed a sitter at least two days a week, and at first it looked like we were in luck. Through a friend we found an older woman who began coming to our apartment to watch our daughter while I went off to the university. Our daughter would cry when I left, but this sitter worked so hard and showed so much concern for our daughter that I felt comfortable, if a bit unhappy, going on about my business. I remember one particular day the sitter was quacking like a duck as I left the apartment, working mightily hard to keep my little daughter happy.

That very same day, though, things fell apart. Our sitter traveled back to her home in a van that carried a whole host of babysitters, handymen, and other workers from one neighborhood to another. The van stopped in front of our building, but my wife wasn't back home yet to take over with our daughter. The van honked and honked, the driver yelled, and not knowing what else to do, the sitter left our one-year-old with the doorman until my wife returned. Bad judgment, to be sure. But in dealing with what to do next, plenty of well-meaning people suggested that we keep this sitter on until we find a replacement. But how could we? She had just proven that in a pinch, she'd make a bad—a potentially dangerous—decision. She couldn't come back. But we had no replacement. The next day, I took our daughter with me to my classes, making no one happy—not my teachers, not my students, and not even my daughter. The only real insight I had was that old phrase—the days are long, but the years are short. I didn't want to make a decision that would shortchange our daughter just because I felt the pressure of those long, long days—the tug of my studies and my teaching work. I decided to abandon some of my classes, to cut out half my workload, and to become the sitter we were looking for.

As the weeks stretched into months, and the months to years—with another daughter added to our family, and then, years later, our son—I had countless days that seemed never to end, frustrations that seemed almost unbearable, and periods when I truly struggled to keep myself going. I remember waking up a few months into my life as the primary child-care parent and wondering how long I could last—maybe a few more months? Maybe a year? Could I go a whole year like this? The days, I knew, would be long.

Today my daughter is, literally, packing her bags for college. Those long days have faded in memory, though the sweetness of being so close with my little girl is still with me. My wife and I have managed to trade off roles, one of us being the full-time parent while the other has gone full bore at work, and it all seems to have worked. We take the perspective of the years now, and we miss those long, long days. But we made decisions that worked for us, with an understanding that time was our most precious commodity. Money could not have bought what our time with our children gave us, and we continue to do our best to make decisions guided by that lesson. Sometimes we grumble and regret that we can't give as much time to our family and friends and others in need as we'd like—work, health, and other obligations still press on us. But whenever there's a real choice, we bend toward the gift of time, toward slowing down and *being there,* literally, for others whenever we can. Because the days are long, but the years . . .

Purpose Steers You Straight

A few years ago I picked up a magazine article about a man I greatly admired, Bob Moses. Moses had been one of the low-profile heroes of the civil rights movement, a man who had taken enormous risks again and again to help African American people in Mississippi register to vote. Moses was beaten, homes he was staying in were bombed, and he was taken off to jail on countless occasions based on groundless charges. Nothing stopped him. He always found his way back to the small streets and dirt roads of 1960s Mississippi, to keep on with his work of registering people to vote.

Moses had been one of very few African American students at Hamilton College in New York State in the 1950s and went from there to Harvard University to study mathematics and philosophy. He had been interested in staying on for a PhD in philosophy, but he found the academic world too far removed from the lives of ordinary people, and the power of ideas to make practical changes in society. He received a master's from Harvard and went on to teach math at a private school in New York City, happy to make a difference in the lives of his students, but growing more impatient to find a way to help in the larger struggle for civil rights that was making more and more front-page news. He left his post as a teacher and went south, to Mississippi.

Moses avoided formal leadership positions. In a movement filled with gifted orators, he didn't like giving speeches and was almost impossible to hear when he did, he spoke so quietly. But day after day, week after week, month after month, Moses worked with people in small Mississippi towns, often in McComb County, to encourage local people to register to vote.

He stood beside them in the county offices as they were laughed at by local officials. He walked beside them as they were turned away from voting places. He stood beside them as they were beaten, and he was beaten, too.

After years of this work, with some real progress made in the form of the historic federal Voting Rights Act of 1965 and growing numbers of African American citizens on the voting rolls, and with some real struggle as the once-cohesive civil rights movement was fragmenting and losing a sense of common purpose, Moses traveled to Africa and lived there for several years, working as a teacher and studying African history and culture. Then he returned to the United States, went back to study at Harvard, and began a remarkable new project, the Algebra Project. Working out of offices in McComb, Mississippi, and Cambridge, Massachusetts, Moses began creating new ways to bring traditional algebra training to middle-school students, particularly African American students. He pointed to the connection between success in school and success later in life—and, more particularly, Moses pointed to algebra, the first great challenge for young people to think abstractly (to think about x, the missing piece in the puzzles of algebra), as the place in the curriculum where far too many young people went off the tracks. If he could help them master the tricky thinking of algebra, he could help them grasp the full lives as citizens they would deserve.

In fact, Moses would regularly talk about the connections between his work in the civil rights movement and his work in the Algebra Project. It was, in many ways, the same work. It was about helping people live the lives they deserved to live, helping them grasp the tools they needed to enjoy the rights and privileges that they deserved to enjoy. His purpose was unchanged, his modest manner was unchanged, and unlike many veterans of the civil rights movement, Moses was not bitter, did not look at his early years as better than his later years, and had no regrets. He was still engaged, still helping others, and still fighting the most morally and socially important struggle he could imagine.

He understood the war he was fighting—for justice, to empower young people too often pushed aside and kept from what they deserved—and was not fooled by the differences in the battles, whether they be battles for voter registration or battles for better education. His method was the same: go out and do some good, go out and help one man register to vote, one child learn algebra, while continuing to talk about the larger issues. He remained both a doer and a thinker and kept on that same path of purpose. And he's still at it today. On many of the Algebra Project's materials, this line comes up again and again—"If we can do it, we should." That captures the spirit of activism in its most positive meaning that drives the project, and that came from the vision of Bob Moses. If we can make a positive difference for others, we should. And here's the best news: we can.

Where Does Purpose Come From?

Living a life of purpose is a choice. We have the choice to strive toward goals that make the world better for others and for ourselves, or not.

There's not much mystery to it—living with a purpose makes life more meaningful, makes the world a better place, and helps you reach your personal goals. But where does purpose come from?

Where Does Purpose Come From?

Plato answered that question with his idea of the forms. The greatest purpose is helping to make life in the world we live in come closer to the perfection of the forms. The feeling you get when you look at your house and say, *It's nice, but not as nice as it should be,* comes from your inner awareness that there is an ideal form the house is striving for. Bringing the imperfect world closer to the perfection of the forms was a natural ambition for Plato, and a deeply satisfying purpose.

Aristotle, Plato's student, focusing more on man's happiness, made the powerful argument that happiness flows from goodness. When we are unhappy, instead of seeking pleasure, we should seek virtue, because happiness is actually a moral state. The better we are as people, the happier we will be. But that still leaves the questions of what, exactly, virtue *is,* and where virtue comes from, unanswered.

Emerson added a powerful psychological logic to the question of purpose when he rewrote his essay "History" after his son had died. His new essay, "Experience," revealed the personal need to find a way out of the hole of depression, and Emerson used that need to craft a philosophy of action: "Up again, old heart!" he wrote. "The true romance which the world exists to realize, will be the transformation of Genius into practical power." He came to understand that if he wished to live a meaningful life again, he'd need to do more than think and feel—he'd need to act, to stand and fight, to cultivate a higher purpose and then go out and change the world. For Emerson, purpose is really a self-invention—it comes from a personal need and is crafted through personal will.

Søren Kierkegaard's version of purpose—what he calls the "leap of faith"—takes Emerson's self-invention a bit further. Like Emerson, Kierkegaard understands that meaningful purpose only comes out of great personal struggle. The individual must make a choice to believe in a purpose, a choice based on personal feeling rather than on logic. If belief and purpose were easy, everyone would have them. But they are hard. Kierkegaard is certain that this difficulty is a test. He has a more explicitly religious view of purpose and sees the leap of faith as a challenge God demands of man, a test of the heart and soul of the individual who seeks meaning in his or her life.

In the final analysis, all of these thinkers are right. Plato's notion that there are such things as perfect beauty and true justice, and that we should aspire to them, is inspiring and helps us stay on track to make the world better. Though we can't hold those perfect ideals in our hands, or know them directly, the passions of the artist and the activist make powerful testimony to the existence of greater things. Aristotle's insight about what makes people happy is powerfully inspiring: what better advice can anyone hear than *be good*? Emerson's crafting of a philosophy after personal tragedy and struggle rings with the truth of lived experience. And Kierkegaard's leap of faith is a test that seems worth any effort to pass. There is a limit to what we can know for sure, and when we cultivate the ability to see and feel a bit beyond what we *know*, we live far better lives.

All of this collective wisdom leaves us with one central lesson, a lesson about the unexpected paths to a life of real purpose: the way to find happiness for yourself is to help others to be happy. This is the irony—the irrationality—of moral discovery: to find your inner self, you need to look outward. Where does purpose come from? It comes from everyone else. It comes from the complex, rich life lived by every stranger you brush against in the street. To be the person you are born to be, you have to look outward, not inward, and ask who *others* are struggling to become. In their struggles and their joys you will find your greatest success and your doorway to the deepest happiness men and women are able to feel.

PART VI

PUTTING IT ALL TOGETHER

What Does Real Success Look Like?

What does it look like when you're on the path to meeting all your goals—getting things right at home, at work, and in your community? The four stories in Chapter 13 of people thinking at the highest level and sharing their strength offer a glimpse.

13

Making the Power of Purpose Work in Your Life

Making It Work at Home: Family

Sam stepped out of the elevator and looked up at the ceiling. He wasn't sure where to go next—out the glass door to the street—and then where? Maybe back upstairs to finish the fight with Sue. After three years of marriage it was hardly the first go-round they'd had. In fact, at times Sam felt that whenever they fought they were always going back to the very same fight, the one they'd started a few months before they were married, the one that went with them everywhere they traveled and every new place they lived. They fought about respect: Sue felt Sam didn't show her enough, criticizing her too often for driving too fast, or leaving the apartment door open or losing her keys. They also fought about money—Sue felt Sam spent too freely and got such a charge of power out of buying things that he didn't think enough about the future, about saving for a house, saving to help when they had a baby, saving for the rainy day that would surely come sometime.

Sam was exhausted. It was just before noon on a Saturday, and he'd hoped to sleep late. But Sue had been up early, cleaning and being generally unhappy since eight. He could feel her mood even before he'd woken up. She was, as people had often told her, a good communicator. Just his luck. She spent half the morning communicating her unhappiness right through his closed eyelids, and the moment he'd gotten up he was already on the losing end of Sue's argument.

Why couldn't he put things away before he went to sleep? Why did they need the big-screen TV staring at them across the bedroom? Why couldn't he be more supportive of her plans to go to graduate school? Why couldn't he be more supportive in general?

He listened, and listened. (Sam took some pride in being a good listener.) But then he just felt himself bubble over. "Why not? Why can't I do more for you? Just look at the way you treat me! I don't need this, and I don't think I deserve this. This relationship is a voluntary association, you know. There's no lock keeping me in here, so I don't know why you think you can just lay into me like this."

With that, Sam left the apartment.

Standing in front of the elevator in the lobby, he looked again at the glass doors to the street and knew he didn't want to leave. Yes, marriage is a voluntary association—Sam was a lawyer and phrases like that appealed to him—but it was more than that, too. He loved Sue, and what he really wanted to do was go back up to the apartment and find the groove they were often in, the one in which he was kind to her and she was kind to him. But he needed a little time to think things through before he could help them both get to where they wanted to be.

Sam thought about why he'd left the apartment. He understood that his pride had been offended. He'd taken Sue's bait and reacted to her in a perfectly human, understandable way— a pure level-one response. He had looked at himself, a young man being yelled at by his wife, and he hadn't liked what he'd seen. He didn't like who he was in that scene.

With that understanding in mind, Sam could climb up a level in his thinking. Now that he was clear about how he had looked to himself—and how that self-view had triggered him to leave his apartment—he asked himself how he must have seemed to Sue. She was obviously unhappy about something more important than his sleeping late, and more important than their television. But he hadn't had a clue and woke up in the middle of a drama already well under way, coming across to Sue, no doubt, as unfeeling. He could see that he must have looked uninterested in Sue's feelings, and that had only made things worse.

But what *were* Sue's feelings? Anger about the big TV? Anger about Sam sleeping late? He doubted that—both issues were really symbols of other issues—bigger issues. He knew Sue was nervous about going back to school at night and confused about what the next few years would hold for them both. If they had a baby, maybe she'd quit her job. Could she stay in school, though? If she stayed in school, would they have enough money for her to be home full time with the baby, too, or would Sue have to juggle school, work, *and* a baby? Could they possibly get that juggling act right?

By now Sam was as confused and concerned as Sue—and that was actually a good thing. He knew what his next few years of work would look like with or without a baby. He had a job he liked in a solid profession, and he was good at it. That anchored him, he realized. It made getting up in the morning a little easier. It also made sleeping late a little easier, too. But it didn't help Sue very much. So he had to do more to help her right now, he thought, and he turned back toward the elevator.

He'd done some vital thinking, thinking through each of the three levels. And now he was ready to look beyond himself and spend some time helping Sue share *her* feelings and clarify *her* goals. He had a purpose now.

In personal relationships, the kind of thinking that this young man practiced—thinking at the third level—is indispensable. You simply can't reach your goals—you can't be a good friend, a good partner, a good spouse, or a good parent—without asking how other people see themselves, and what *their* goals are.

By nature, we think at the first level, concerned about our own feelings and identities above all else. When people we care about ask for things we're not in the habit of giving—when they push us in ways we haven't been pushed before—our natural reaction is often to push back, to protect ourselves, to put up defenses. Getting to the next level requires personal discipline. It takes practice to ask, How do I look to others? What role am I playing in *their* story? Even more important is getting to the level beyond, the third level, asking, What does this other person care most about? What's on her mind? What's the shape of her own personal story right now? Sam asked the right questions, and just in time. He would regret walking out that door—and though he's got lots of work yet to do to support

Sue, he's on the way to having the kind of partnership with her that will sustain them both for many years.

MAKING IT WORK ON THE JOB: SELLING

Sally B. is one of the greatest salespeople I've ever seen. She's incredibly smart, but not complicated. When you talk to her, you never scratch your head feeling like she knows something you don't. Instead you feel like she helps you rise up to her own high level of insight and understanding. Just being with her makes you feel smarter and more powerful.

On a typical day, Sally makes five or six sales calls on behalf of a small ($20 million in sales) technology-products firm that sells tools for tracking inventory and preventing theft from warehouses and offices. Sally estimates that in every big-city office building, she's probably got at least a couple of dozen prospective accounts. "The world is my oyster," she says. "I've got a great product at a fair price, and most businesses need it, even if they don't know it yet."

Sally likes to start her day at the foundation of the pyramid: with ambition. Though she's officially a senior sales executive without formal responsibilities for supervising other salespeople, Sally enjoys checking in with some of her junior colleagues every morning. Most of them have spent training days riding along with Sally on calls, and she gets a kick out of staying in close touch—and razzing them a bit about their numbers. "It's about keeping your jets hot—staying competitive, staying in game mode," Sally says. So she calls a very aggressive young rep and shouts into the phone, "Hey! It's eight o'clock! How much money'd you make so far today?" She laughs, he laughs, and they share the news of a colleague's big sale to a major department store. "Awesome news," Sally says. "Let's go make some more."

Then comes Sally's first call for the day—or her first non-call, actually. "This one's a pass," she says, flipping through a prospect folder. She's done her homework on this company and knows that it'll be cash poor for the year, but is scheduled for an infusion of capital in about eighteen months. "I've got a competitor who makes a product that's not as good as mine—it won't last, and their service stinks. But it's adequate and costs half as much. So I've sent this CEO a note advising him to go with the competitor for now—they'll preserve more of their cash that way and get to their eighteen-month infusion point with less risk. By around then, my competitor's weaknesses will be all too apparent, and I'll be ready to make the long-term sale. But today, I've got nothing for them. If I were them, I wouldn't buy from me today, and that's what I told them."

Sally's next prospect is actually an existing account. It's a four-store electronics chain, and she sells it radio tags for expensive inventory. From a central PC, the store owner can see where every piece of tagged inventory is. Sally's visit coincides with an uncomfortable discovery at the flagship store. A $3,800 music synthesizer now seems to be tucked into a new location—the apartment of an employee. Sally knows the right office at the police department to handle getting the music machine back, and she calls her contact there (she's been through similar adventures with other customers). She then hands her cell phone to the store owner, who reports the crime. He's treated well by Sally's police contact. On her way out, as the owner thanks her for her help, she tells him about a new kind of radio tag that will call into the store, or to a beeper, without needing to be prompted from the central PC. She'd like to come by the next day for a demo. The owner happily agrees, and Sally pencils it into her datebook as she heads to her car.

Next comes a deal to be closed. A large insurance company has a regional office with about two hundred staff in town. The company loses about a thousand dollars per employee per year in theft and other "shrinkage," a hefty total of $200,000. Sally's promised that she can cut that number by more than half. The cost will be about $25,000 a year, and Sally's pushing for a three-year deal. She understands the client's need and doesn't think she's got any direct competitor bidding on the deal. The only real barrier is trust—she needs to build some, but she also needs to get a signed contract and wants to accelerate the trust building. So she takes two steps to get over her client's reluctance to enter into a three-year deal. She's using level-three thinking to her advantage, asking herself, what does the client here want? What are his goals and his fears?

Those questions lead her to specific actions. First she tells the prospect exactly what she's thinking and shares that, were she in his shoes, she'd want to do the deal but would be a little nervous about the multiyear term.

Then she takes out her cell phone and calls the president of a regional bank in town. The bank is a client, too, and she'd arranged for the president to be available to take the call as a favor and sing her praises. Then she proposes that the three-year contract have a ninety-day exit clause—something that could cost her some real money, because she'd never recoup her start-up costs if the deal went south ninety days after starting. But Sally knows that to earn trust, you have to show trust, so she uses that risk as the lever to get the deal. They all shake hands, and Sally feels great. She makes a note in her book to call the new-account installation group at her office, and then she takes a few moments to enjoy the wash of positive emotion that always follows a clean close.

Having earned her pay for the day with that deal, Sally makes three cold calls before heading back to the office—two in the same building as the insurance company, and one between the insurance company building and her office. In all three cases, she follows her usual MO—she gives her card to the receptionist, asks what the best times might be to find the office manager or loss-prevention manager in person, collects their names and whatever information about their schedules she can, and then asks whether there might be a chance to see them before she leaves. One out of three is a hit—she gets into the office of the loss-prevention manager and introduces herself. She pitches a lunch-and-demo and says she'll call in a few days to try to schedule something, after the manager has had time to look through the folder of information she leaves behind.

One of the other cold calls leads her to the office manager's assistant, and the other leads nowhere—she drops her folder of information with the receptionist and expects it will probably wind up in the trash. But you never know. That's what she was thinking on her way out, at the close of a good day—you never know, but you always try. She's totally focused on doing what it takes to win at her work; that's her purpose when she puts on her work clothes. And she knows exactly what it takes: helping other people solve their problems. Every day she solves a problem for someone else, she earns another dollar, she makes another friend, and she leaves the world a little better than she found it.

Making It Work on the Job: Managing

After three years of work at American Aero, Bob A. was facing a day that would make or break his career as a senior VP of the $200 million transportation services company. When Bob had joined AA three years earlier, he'd found a solid organization with a number of weak spots. Bob, who was a few years out of business school, had enough experience to spot problems and enough patience to wait for just the right time to solve them for the long term. He'd decided to let go a weak regional VP a year ago and was now about to hire his replacement. The two final candidates for the spot were coming in for their second interviews.

That covered Bob's early morning—eight till ten. At 10:30, he'd be meeting with AA's founder and chairman to present his plans for restructuring the company's customer service operation (though Bob thought "restructuring" was too kind a word— "creating" the customer service operation might be more accurate). At noon, Bob was visiting a Fortune 100 client. At three, he had an hour of thinking and planning time scheduled. At four, he'd be meeting with his regional VPs, and at six, he would stop into the after-school program he helped to fund, to chat with some of the parents as they came by to pick up their kids.

A busy day, but no busier than usual. What really made the day important were the key decisions he'd have to make— choosing the right regional VP, and making the right approach to the CEO on the big customer-service project. If he could get both right, Bob would be moving decisively toward success.

The two final candidates for the VP job were both strong contenders. They had each held the right kinds of jobs and had made strong impressions on Bob and on the other regional VPs he'd had them speak with. Bob's agenda for these final meetings was clear: he wanted to get a peek into their minds. He wanted to know how good a job each naturally did of trying to understand other people.

A true believer in level-three thinking, Bob was already pretty clear about each of the candidate's goals for themselves. They were both ambitious and good at learning new skills. Now he wanted to see whether either one had the level-three instinct and would use a final interview to try to understand Bob better. That would make all the difference in the future, Bob thought—the candidate who proved better able to appreciate how other people saw their own goals would get the job.

Angela Smith was the first candidate to come in, and she came off like a winner. She arrived a few minutes early, looked rested and sharp, and had an easy though alert manner. "Well," Bob began, "I'm really delighted to have you here. As you know, we're very close to making a decision. I wanted you to have a last chance to ask me questions today, though, so here we are, and I'm all yours." Bob knew this was something of a curveball. Angela was indeed a bit surprised—she had imagined that Bob would be asking the questions, at least some of them. But she quickly found a good groove. "Well," she began, unconsciously copying Bob's own conversation opener, "my first question would be how you think the search for your new colleague has gone so far. Has the process met your goals?" "It's been a good process," Bob responded. "I think we had some strong candidates in, and we're close to making a great hire."

"What do you think the first great accomplishments of a great new VP would be in, say, six months?"

"Hmm," Bob responded, thinking hard, "six months isn't

long for accomplishments. I'd have to say, though, that at six months the new VP should be totally up and running, doing less learning about our company and more learning about our clients. So I suppose that first great accomplishment I'd want to see is the learning about who we are and how we work. After that the new VP can start hitting long balls and scoring runs."

"What would a long ball well hit look like?" Angela asked in response, and Bob talked a bit about a recent project one of his other regional VPs had landed and managed.

"And how about you, Bob, if I may," Angela then asked. "What are your goals here at American Aero for the next year or so?" The conversation went on for most of the next hour, and at the end, Bob was pleased. Angela had listened well, asked questions about *his* goals, and was clearly thinking at the third level, thinking about how she'd be able to help other people reach *their* goals as part of her own plans for success.

The other candidate, John Goodman, was also an excellent interview, though he was a bit wobbly at the beginning, obviously surprised by the agenda for the day's meeting. Unlike Angela, John came up with questions that reflected details of American Aero's business—mostly ground that had been covered in earlier, more structured interviews—and didn't seem to be as skillful in listening to Bob's conversational cues. Certainly John was less concerned about figuring out Bob's goals than he was about putting himself on display. John was too focused on how he looked to Bob, instead of focusing on Bob's own goals for the meeting, and for the long term. John was at level two. And that, finally, was what won Angela the job—the fact that she seemed more naturally attuned to other people's concerns and goals. She was a level-three thinker.

Bob had his role reversed in his next meeting, with his boss, the chairman of AA. He'd be the supplicant in this meeting, not the power player. He walked into Al Smith's office and shook hands with the chairman warmly. Bob understood that AA had lots of opportunity to do a better job managing customer interactions and building in more structure to their communications with new and existing customers. Al didn't see things quite the same way. His outlook was more personality driven—hire the right people to run customer service, people with great empathy for others, great knowledge of the business, and strong follow-through, and customer service would take care of itself. So far, this strategy had worked. It had built AA into a $200 million company and made Al richer than he'd ever thought he'd be.

So how would Bob help Al see beyond his current vision? He began this way: "Al, if you don't mind, can I ask you a couple of questions to frame what I'm about to suggest?" "Sure," the chairman replied. Bob then asked two questions: first, What should our goals be for customer service at AA? and second, How should we measure our success in reaching these goals? Al had a range of answers—no customer complaints, increased sales tied to customer service visits, high scores on third-party service audits. The bottom line, though, was that Al wanted a reputation for service that beat his main rivals, and he wanted hard data to prove it. Once Al had put these answers on the table, Bob was able to present his ideas for customer service in terms of Al's own vision. He was able to present his new ideas as tools for reaching the goals that Al believed in, to make the details look like the logical extensions of Al's ambitions.

As the meeting wound down Al asked for Bob to put it all on paper. Al obviously liked what he had heard and was energized by the specifics Bob had added to his own less-than-focused sense of doing something big in customer service. Bob left the meeting feeling like he was helping Al take his company up to the next level—a good feeling.

Bob's visit to his Fortune 100 client was actually similar to his meeting with Al—and, he thought upon reflection, similar to all his meetings this day. It was about listening to the other guy, understanding his goals, and looking for opportunities to help. Bob needed to hear about some specific issues in AA's engagement with this major client—the customer's perception of quality, his team's responsiveness, and business variables that might shift the overall project plan—but the same basic questions were at the heart of his discussion: How are things doing from your perspective? What are your goals? How can we help you meet them? The meeting was a good one. Some surprises came up, but each new problem had a reasonable enough solution, and the bond between the customer's point man and Bob continued to be strong, based on the feeling that they were each helping the other meet his goals. School ties or hours on the golf course couldn't come close to matching the value of that positive bond.

Back at the office, Bob got ready for his phone conference with his regional VPs. As it began, he reported on his meeting with the two job candidates—the new hire would become a peer member of this group—and then they went round-robin for updates on business operations and a little brainstorming on some problems that were popping up in a couple of locations.

The five regional VPs had a certain level of trust, though there was real competitive juice flowing, too. Bob felt OK with that as long as it stayed positive, and as long as everyone understood that the best way to reach their personal goals was to help the company as a whole meet its key targets. Toward that end,

Bob held part of the bonus pool for the VPs in a discretionary account, and let the VPs set one big goal for the group to trigger everyone getting their share of that extra money. The ground rules for this bonus money were that the trigger had to be measurable—like total sales, or total growth over a certain benchmark—but it also had to reflect genuine teamwork among the VPs.

This year that set-aside bonus was triggered by sales improvement in a couple of large national accounts all the VPs had to work on. Without being careful, Bob might find that each VP would only service the account activity for the big national accounts in their own regions; but the bonus encouraged them to spend some time every quarter working on strategy to improve service at a higher level. The money was significant enough—about a third of all bonus compensation—that this was more than a game. This was where Bob put the firm's money where his mouth was. If he believed in teamwork, he needed to pin money on it, he felt.

The collaboration on the big national accounts helped in other ways, too—not only because the VPs got used to working together, but also because they had a better understanding of one another's strengths and weaknesses from all that collaboration. They did a better job working together not only because of increased trust built from winning some victories together, but also because they knew more about who in their group was better at what.

After the VP call, Bob took stock of his day. As the light faded outside his office windows, he felt he'd earned his pay. He'd found the right regional VP for the open slot, and he had taken the first steps toward a big win rebuilding AA's customer service operation. His VP team was cooking along just fine, and he was wrapping up at a decent hour—just in time to swing by the City Prep after-school program on his way home.

City Prep was an urban charter school with tough entrance requirements and a pool of talented middle-school and high-school kids mostly from poor families. A buddy of Bob's taught there and had gotten to telling Bob about some of the families at the school a few years ago. Not all the families were models of hope—too many parents made bad decisions in their own lives, didn't support their children well, and seemed to take two steps back for everyone step forward. A student would win a scholarship to an elite summer camp, but then the family would pull up and move—or a parent would take off and throw the family into crisis. But plenty of the families were classic strivers, pushing hard to get through every day on lousy job wages while getting their kids on track for college. Bob's buddy wanted to start an after-school center for the middle schoolers, who particularly needed extra support. Keep them in school till their parents got home, Bob's friend told him, and at least some will stay on the right path. The program would cost about $2,000 a month. Bob, a single man earning over $100,000 a year, signed up to pay for a third of the cost. The school found the rest of the money from other donors, and a few months ago the center had opened. Bob liked to stop by now and then, to see his money at work and to enjoy the feeling of helping others.

MAKING IT WORK AT HOME: COMMUNITY

Emerson Street sits a few blocks away from the Third Avenue School. The closer you get to the school, the fancier the homes get. Emerson Street is close enough that there's not too much concern about crime, and most of the houses are pretty well kept up. One block closer to the school, though, and the homes are all lovely without a single exception, all freshly painted, all the yards carefully watered and trimmed and filled with flowers.

The Emerson Street neighbors want their street to be more like the next street over, a little neater, a bit more lovely, and regarded by the rest of the community as being on the right side of town. Right now, many felt that they were seen as being *almost* on the right side. The main problem, most of them agreed, was the Wagner house. Mrs. Wagner had lived there for fifty years and was a fixture on the block, even if she was seldom seen. She spent most of her days sitting on her back porch, sipping tea and watching her garden. A caretaker came by twice a day to check in on her and serve her two hot meals. Someone from the neighborhood would trim her bushes a couple of times a year, and beyond that the neighborhood paid her little attention. Most of the others were much younger; several had school-age children. Mrs. Wagner must have been over eighty.

Every year, Emerson Street stopped traffic and held a block party. The kids played in the middle of the street. Half a dozen grills were wheeled into a horseshoe in front of the Golds, and well into the night people sat around on their lawn chairs talking over everything from property taxes to presidential politics.

This year, everyone was excited because a house on the next block had sold for half a million dollars. Things were certainly looking up for the neighborhood, they all agreed. But their block was underperforming, a few thought. It didn't quite have that quality they all wanted it to have, didn't quite *say* what they wanted their block to say.

Everyone was polite, more or less, but they all knew that Mrs. Wagner's house was a problem. It badly needed a paint job. The gutters were sagging. It just looked shabby. "Can we talk to her?" someone asked. "Been tried," someone else answered. "Last year Bob Kennedy went over there and asked her to please put some money into the paint job, but she said she just couldn't afford it and didn't feel it was really necessary, anyway."

Hearing that, a few of the neighbors sitting in the gathering dark in front of their warm grills looked around, wondering how to respond, taking in the responses of the others. No one offered any direct criticism of Mrs. Wagner, but no one said anything else either. "Well," Fred Gold finally said, "I understand her health isn't the best. I certainly don't want to be the one to ask her again this year. I don't think any one of us wants to be the bad guy, eh? I mean, is it really worth it?"

Angie Brown exhaled slowly. She wasn't angry, maybe a little sad. "I just don't know," she said. "I really want to see this work out well. Imagine how people feel when they drive down this block, and they see such nice houses—your house, Fred, and the Kennedys', and I think ours is looking very nice, and then that old house just sitting there with its rotten peeling paint and all that crabgrass. It's just not good for a soul for that house to be sitting there like that. Not good for anyone."

No one had much else to say on the matter. The kids began chasing fireflies, the mosquitoes began to bite, and soon enough the grills were tipped up onto their wheels and the annual party was over. There wasn't much accomplished in the discussion about Mrs. Wagner, but Bob Kennedy began thinking about how he could make a positive difference.

The next day, he stopped by Mrs. Wagner's just as the lady came to help her with breakfast. He guessed that Mrs. Wagner might not be able to come to the door, but if he timed it right, she'd have her helper there. To his surprise, though, Mrs. Wagner answered the door herself, and she seemed glad to have Bob there. "Well, well," she said. "I haven't seen you for some time." She invited him out to her back porch, and they shared some tea. Bob told Mrs. Kennedy that the neighbors were planning some projects in the neighborhood and asked her if she had any ideas for improving the street. She didn't seem happy with that question. Bob felt badly right away; Mrs. Wagner realized he'd been testing her out, to see if she'd be willing to ask for help with her house, and she'd been insulted. She stood up and said "You know, it's lovely to have a visitor. I don't have many. I don't think I can help you with your neighborhood problems, but I do hope you'll come again." And that was the end of the visit.

Bob told Fred Gold and Angie Brown about the visit a few days later, and they all puzzled over the best way to proceed. It was Angie who put into words what they had all been wondering. "What do you think she really wants?" None of the neighbors could answer that question, but they set about to find out. After years of having no visitors from the neighborhood at all, Mrs. Wagner began to see new faces at her door every other day or so. She certainly enjoyed the attention and began keeping a pot of tea on the stove just in case someone would stop in.

After a few weeks, the neighbors were no closer to understanding what Mrs. Wagner really wanted, but they had all begun to enjoy hearing her stories about the neighborhood during World War II, the blackouts of the 1950s and 1960s, and the time Ronald Reagan came to town and passed by the corner in his limousine, the whole block entirely packed with people who'd come by to wave.

"Well," Angie said to Bob Kennedy one afternoon while they were both out watching parents walking the street with their toddlers, "I wonder whether she's tired of us yet. She seems to like having us all visit, but I get the feeling she's a little suspicious. And maybe she should be. I think I'm going to invite her over to tea today at my house. Maybe a change in perspective is what's really needed here."

And that, it turned out, did the trick. Angie and her two-year-old son took Mrs. Wagner for a walk across the street to their house and made her Earl Grey tea, which she enjoyed. Then they sat on Angie's front porch and chatted about the neighborhood's goings-on back during the Carter administration. All the while, Mrs. Wagner had a long look at her shabby home. Before she stood to leave, she said quietly, "I simply had no idea." And two weeks later, a crew arrived to start painting the Wagner house.

Mrs. Wagner had arrived at the third level of thinking and understood what her neighbors had wanted all along. Her neighbors, in turn, realized that they had failed to see the world through Mrs. Wagner's eyes. Those eyes had never seen what that old house looked like—they had only looked outward. It took a visit across the street and some Earl Grey tea to complete the picture they saw, and once that broader picture was clear, action followed soon enough.

AFTERWORD
A DREAM FOR MY CHILDREN

EVERY NOW AND THEN ONE OF MY THREE CHILDREN WRITES a paper for school or a private note, on my laptop computer, knowing, I'm sure, that I'll find it there and enjoy peeking into it. As I was finishing work on this book, one of my daughters wrote an essay for school called "Dreams for My Future." And it was just as lovely for a parent to read as you might imagine— she dreams of becoming a reporter (like her mother); she dreams of making a difference in other people's lives; she dreams of seeing the world; she dreams of staying close to her friends and family.

Thinking about my daughter's dreams as I've been finishing up work on *The Power of Purpose* has led me to think about the future and to picture my three children living lives of purpose, developing the habit of seeing the world through the eyes of others, and making a positive difference in the lives of as many people as possible. The ideas at the center of this book are ideas that I hope will have some impact on their lives. And, in fact, they've each embraced these ideas in some small and large ways already.

Ambition

My son, the youngest of our three children, joined my wife and me last summer at Amherst College, where we were helping to lead a summer Great Books program for middle-school and high-school students. He was very impressed by the lectures about Homer's *Odyssey* that he'd overheard. He loved the idea of Odysseus, the king of the Greek island nation of Ithaca, struggling to find his way back home to his family after his service in the Trojan War. For ten years, Odysseus fights his way through rough seas that Poseidon, the angry sea god, puts in his way; he resists the temptations of the Sirens who try to lure him from his path; he fights the one-eyed Cyclops, and innumerable other beasts, men, and forces of nature pushing against his purpose of returning home, embracing his family, and putting away his sword to live a life of peace. Through it all, he never gives up and stays steadfast on his personal path.

My son loved hearing about his adventures and loved even more the idea of a man who never gives up. As he took up mountain climbing in the months after our summer with Homer—dragging his poor father along with him—his refrain was "I never give up," straight out of *The Odyssey*. If I heard him say that once in the climbing gym or clambering up a boulder, I heard him say it a hundred times. Homer's ambition and steadfastness inspired him, and he understood what is to hold to a purpose and hold to a dream.

I've seen my older daughter, now seventeen, show real ambition, too. When she was determined to make her school's basketball team, she dragged me to the court every day after work for a solid month, and I saw her teach herself the discipline of the game. She signs up for stacks of courses—and local leadership roles—and extra school projects—and sports teams, to the point that she comes home exhausted. But she doesn't give up. Most impressive, I've seen her take harder courses that she can't get the highest grades in, because she knows she'll learn more in those courses, and she values the substance of her education more than the easy grades that would give her more glitter on her transcripts. She's got a vision of what she wants to take from school and what she wants to give to others at this point in her life, and she's sticking to it.

My middle daughter, a high-achieving student and disciplined athlete, continues to impress everyone in our house with how hard she pushes herself on all fronts. When I was a teenager, it didn't take much encouragement for me to put down my school books, or take a day off from an after-school obligation. My middle daughter sees the world differently. Every class and every team she's on represents a promise she's determined to keep, and look out if you try to get in her way. She wants to achieve a tremendous amount, and she puts up a fierce fight to achieve her ambitions.

I dream that my children will hold tight to their ambitions, that they will not compromise on their hopes and plans to be truly good people and to achieve great things. Like all parents, I wish I could remain by their side every day, guiding them and reminding them of how truly powerful they are. But of course I can't—our very success in helping our children grow into independent people is what draws them from our side and launches them out into their world, beyond the sounds of our voices. What we taught them in those early years when they were always underfoot, when we talked with them every hour of every day, will help them find their way. Among the lessons I hope to have taught my three in those early years—lessons I try to reinforce as they grow older—are the lessons of big dreams, of setting the bar high and leaping with all their might to clear it. How wonderful to watch them reach for their great ambitions.

Insight

"First," my son said, "I'll climb the little mountain. Then I'll climb the big one."

"It makes me so sad," my middle daughter said, speaking about one of her friends, "to think about how hard it is for her to deal with the problems in her family."

"I want to go on the trip," my older daughter said, talking about a glitzy youth-group weekend study trip, "but if I skip the trip, I know I'll be able to put more time into the other things I'm doing and get more out of them."

With these comments, my children demonstrated that they already grasp some of the important insights for living meaningful lives and finding success. My son understands, even at a young age, the need to walk his chosen path one step at a time. My middle daughter understands how to empathize and see the world through the eyes of others. My oldest daughter understands how to emphasize the war and not be distracted by trying to win every battle. She'd love to take that weekend trip, have fun and learn some things, but she's got a higher-level perspective and thinks about the whole picture of her studies and her life. She's unusually smart about staying in balance and giving up a bit of fun today for the sake of a stronger plan for more learning and more fun next week and next month and next year.

My oldest also has a great sense of balancing the center and the fringe—of blending the creative, free spirit of the rebel with the wisdom of the mainstream. We've spent the past few months visiting colleges, thinking about where she'll want to enroll when she finishes high school in a year. She's weighed some of the tempting options—the schools with a high fun factor, with total freedom, with a culture of rebellion and indulgence—against some more challenging, less-fun places to study, and she has said that she'd like to go somewhere fun, but not too fun; with a touch of the wild, but not too wild. I'm impressed with her judgment, as I often am—this is a young woman with a great understanding of what she needs from the world, and what the world needs from her. She's put herself on a path leading to an outstanding and serious education—at least a little bit fun, but not *too* fun.

RELATIONSHIPS

Here's a little secret: my children fight with one another. Not all the time, but too often for my taste. They yell and scream every now and then, and it drives my wife and me crazy. But every now and then something happens when they're at the height of a nasty exchange, and they snap back into what I like to think of as their real personalities—they help one another, they communicate quickly and thoughtfully, and they get done what needs to get done. It might be on a weekend in the country, when they've been fighting over who gets to use the bathroom, and then one spots a big bug crawling across the floor. They put aside the foolish fighting and make a plan in seconds—*You get the bucket! I'll get some big paper! You run to the door and get ready to slam it shut!* Then one gets the bug to crawl on the paper, the other dumps it into the bucket, gets the bucket out the door, and the third slams the door shut while they collapse in the laughter of relief, the little monster expelled from the house and teamwork rediscovered as a true joy.

Their fights are relics of childhood—they grow beyond them as they grow older. They learn lessons every day about how to deal with people, how to express love and concern, how to achieve challenging goals, and how to help others. These lessons draw them further and further away from the pettiness of small children while helping to preserve the sense of fun and wonder that too many adults sacrifice along the way.

I dream for my children that they will learn the lessons of relationships—to share every gain in their lives, to look around themselves and feel lucky for all the good they have, and to find ways to share their good fortune with others. I dream for them that they'll learn that they need to stay close to the people they care the most about, and that they should always be thinking about building teams with friends and strangers, taking those lessons of expelling bugs from the house and applying them to bigger adventures in the world.

I know they've already grasped the value of giving and teaching—they love helping other people, and that makes me incredibly happy. I've seen my seven-year-old son come home from school bursting with pride because he spent the day helping the boy in his class who doesn't talk to anybody learn a bit of what the teacher was teaching and found as a reward a quiet "thank you" from his new friend. To be the one person in the class this gentle but otherwise silent boy will talk to is a badge of honor for my son, and proof that giving—spending time helping this boy during a free period rather than, say, running around the school yard—often feels so much better than taking.

I've seen my middle daughter teach a teammate a small lesson—a trick to get your softball bat leveling off at the end of your swing, or how to see where the goalie expects the soccer ball by looking quickly in her eyes—and I've seen the wonderful fact that she takes just as much pleasure from the glory her friends earn as she does from her own hits and goals.

I've seen that transcendent smile on my oldest daughter's face when she's bent low to hold the hand of a small child, wiped a tear from a little person's face, and felt the incredible warmth of hugging a baby cousin or a day-camper missing her mother, feeling the little arms hug in return, calming sniffles inside the embrace. My daughter gets that moment—she understands that there is nothing better than offering that kind of comfort, no taste, no personal gain, no scratching of an itch that can possibly feel as good. And she gets the connection between how good those things feel and how good they are. She has already learned Aristotle's lesson that the key to being happy lies in being good. For that I'm grateful.

My dream for my children is that as they grow, they never lose sight of how good it is to help others, to share every gain, to be part of teams, and, always, to reach out and connect. There is no way to be as happy or as good standing alone as we can be when we stand close to others. I dream that my children will always know this and always find ways to be good friends, good neighbors, and good givers of those hugs that some of us need so much now and then.

POSITIVE IMPACT

Every so often when my family goes on a hike, we take an empty plastic bag with us to collect whatever trash we find along the way. We've done the same in other places we've lived, particularly when we rented a home in a lovely seaside community in Massachusetts, where a bicycle path sat on the other side of our street, sometimes attracting soda cans and candy wrappers in the tall grass. After a trip across the street with an empty trash bag and a kid or two, for days to come I'd see that little flash of pride in my children's faces as we walked by the bike path that was now free of garbage.

Cleaning up other people's messes doesn't always feel like the right thing to do, but to see a small corner of the world made better because of your own labor is a wonderful thing, and a powerful lesson for a child. The good feelings my children have felt as they looked at a bit of natural beauty that they have helped, in some very small way, to preserve and enhance still live on inside them. Through these small acts they have learned that they are powerful—that they can make a difference. And they have experienced that great irony—that helping others makes you feel so good. Being a little bit selfless brings more good feelings than the most selfish actions ever can.

I dream for my children that they hold tight to these lessons, and that they always look for opportunities to help other people and have a positive impact on the world. I dream that they remember the lessons from the poems of Alexander Pope and

William Carlos Williams. From Pope, I hope they will take the lesson that "Man, like the generous vine, supported lives; / The strength he gains is from the embrace he gives." And from Williams, I hope they see that forgiveness is a powerful form of love, that when they face the inevitable compromises that come from living with others, they'll remain generous and feel happy for the pleasures that other people feel—husbands, wives, children, good friends, even strangers.

"Forgive me," Williams writes in his poem "This Is Just to Say." Forgive me for taking something from you, the voice of the poem asks. Forgive me for stealing a small pleasure that rightly belonged to you, for eating those plums that were in the icebox. "Forgive me. / / They were delicious. / So sweet / and so cold." The voice speaking in this poem asks for forgiveness and understands that it will come, because this is the voice of love speaking, the voice of a life shared with others. This is how a shared life works—I forgive you, and you forgive me, and we forgive each other. We eat the sweet, cold plums and savor them. And most important, if you instead of me eat the plums today, while I might want to poke you with a sharp stick for swiping my sweet, cold fruit, I also share your pleasure, and I'm happy you've had that pleasure. Indeed, in some ways, I'm even happier than I'd be if I'd eaten them myself, because I now have the privilege of forgiving you, a powerfully good and satisfying thing for me to do.

A friend told me a story about his life as a magazine publisher recently that captures the same spirit. He'd launched a new magazine a few years ago and then left the publishing company when a better offer came along. The fellow who replaced him as publisher of that magazine was not gracious—he blamed my friend for any number of difficulties that the magazine faced, few of which were actually my friend's fault. Then one day an invitation arrived in my friend's mailbox, from the editor he'd hired for the magazine who'd stayed on with the new publisher. They were having a party to celebrate five years of successful publication, and my friend was invited. How lovely, he thought. They want me to come. They've gotten beyond the silly politics of my departure and my replacement's maneuvers. So he replied that he'd be delighted to come, bought a plane ticket to fly from his new home to the old magazine's offices for the shindig, and savored the good feelings of reconnecting with the fine publication he'd helped to bring into the world. Then, about a week before the big day, his friend the editor called with a pained voice and said that word had come down to him that the magazine's future would be compromised if my friend showed up at the party. The new publisher didn't want him there, and the editor was doing his dirty work. It was a painful call.

A few months later, my friend found himself only a few blocks from the magazine's office while on a business trip, and on impulse he called his friend the editor and they met at a café to share a cup of coffee. The editor was relieved that my friend was being such a good sport, and the two old friends enjoyed reconnecting. As their visit was winding to a close, my friend thanked the editor: "You gave me a great gift, you know." The editor was puzzled—he knew he'd been the bad guy with that lousy phone call. What was my friend thinking? "You gave me the chance to forgive you. And I do. And I'm so glad to see you." They hugged and went on their ways. "Forgive me," the poet wrote, knowing how great a gift that plum stealer was giving to the person who, now, had the privilege of becoming the forgiver. There is no better way to share our strength with people we care about.

Afterword

I dream for my children that they will continue to see how good it is to give back something every day, to express gratitude for the privileges and pleasures of our lives. I dream that they will look every day for ways to make life a little better for other people they care about, and for strangers, too. And I hope they'll remember those lessons about forgiveness, that they won't hold on to grudges but will understand, instead, how lucky we are to be able to forgive, and how much we gain from forgiving. Because life is too short and too sweet for us to withhold forgiveness from anyone who can use it. We are, after all, lucky to be here.

Nineteenth-century American poet Walt Whitman wrote in his poem "Song of Myself," "Behold, I do not give lectures or a little charity, / When I give I give myself." Whitman, already well known in New York and New England when he wrote these words, could earn a fair paycheck giving lectures or reading his poetry. Occasionally he had enough money in his pocket to give to people on the street with their hands outstretched. And he did lecture, sharing some wisdom. And he did read his poems in large and small halls, sharing some joy. But he knew that his greatest gifts would be gifts of himself—gifts of listening more than talking, of walking beside the beggar more than putting a coin in the beggar's hand. And that is, perhaps, my greatest dream for my children: that as they grow older, like Whitman, when they give, they give themselves.

ABOUT THE AUTHOR

Peter Temes teaches literature humanities in the core curriculum at Columbia University and is the academic director of the Great Books Summer Reading Program at Amherst College and Stanford University. He has served as president of the Great Books Foundation and, until recently, as president of the Antioch New England Graduate School. Peter publishes regularly on ethics, education, and literature in the *New York Times*, *San Francisco Chronicle*, and elsewhere. He lectures around the world and is the author and editor of several books, including *The Just War*, *Against School Reform*, and *Teaching Leadership*. He has taught at Harvard University, the New School for Social Research, and the University of Chicago. He holds a PhD from Columbia University.